WORDSWORTH'S STYLE

Wordsworth's Style

Figures and Themes in the
Lyrical Ballads of 1800

ROGER N. MURRAY

UNIVERSITY OF NEBRASKA PRESS · LINCOLN

Publishers on the Plains
UNP

Copyright © 1967 by the University of Nebraska Press
Library of Congress Catalog Card Number 67–13152

Manufactured in the United States of America

To Elaine

Contents

Acknowledgments

I am grateful to Geoffrey H. Hartman, who illuminated for me the dark inscrutable workmanship of Wordsworth and who read my manuscript; his readers will know that he may not be charged with the shortcomings of this study. I am also indebted to Clark Griffith and Ralph Freedman for their continuing criticism and encouragement, and to Archibald Coolidge, Jr., W. R. Irwin, Donald C. Bryant, and Robert Wachal for their valuable suggestions concerning my style, as well as Wordsworth's.

I am obliged, further, to those librarians at the University of Iowa, the University of Minnesota, and the Wisconsin State University at Eau Claire who helped me obtain the books I needed.

Chapter V, "Synecdoche in 'Michael,'" appeared in *ELH (A Journal of English Literary History)*, December, 1965, and is included here with the kind permission of the editors.

ROGER N. MURRAY

WORDSWORTH'S STYLE

Introduction

⌒

Wordsworth once called language the incarnation and not the dress of thought.[1] Unfortunately, there exists as yet no settled terminology with which the critic can discuss intelligibly the difference between an incarnate word and a merely decorative one. To call the one imaginative and the other fanciful would illuminate things only for Coleridgeans. Two recent suggestions from Wordsworth scholars, however, indirectly raise the question posed by Wordsworth's remark in a new way. The first, from M. H. Abrams, applies to Coleridge, but is relevant here:

> ... almost all the examples of the secondary, or "re-creative" imagination which Coleridge explicitly cites in his criticism would fall under the traditional headings of simile, metaphor, and (in the supreme instances) personification.[2]

The second suggestion, from John Jones, is that certain of Wordsworth's metaphors might be termed "reality-

[1] "Essay Upon Epitaphs," in Nowell C. Smith (ed.), *Wordsworth's Literary Criticism* (London: Henry Frowde, 1905), pp. 126–129.

[2] Meyer H. Abrams, *The Mirror and the Lamp: Romantic Theory and the Critical Tradition* (London: Oxford University Press, 1953), p. 292.

I

metaphors."[3] Were it possible to tell the difference between the traditional metaphor and the "reality-metaphor," the terms incarnate and imaginative, applied to language, would perhaps prove to be useful critical terms indeed. Jones's term draws attention to an implied historical change, when we arrive at Wordsworth, concerning the relationships among words, things, and ideas. Colin C. Clarke, in his study *Romantic Paradox*, treats of these relationships, as they exist in Wordsworth's poetry, in greater detail than does Jones. Clarke's purpose is ostensibly to trace in Wordsworth such terms as "image," "form," and "sensation," but these terms lead him to others, all of which appear to him to be grounded in Wordsworth on an epistemological paradox and to be simultaneously metaphoric and literal:

> Because an attempt is made . . . to create a world in which the dimensions are, indifferently, spatial and mental, the word "prolong" takes on a more-than-metaphoric force:
>
> > See common forms prolong the endless chain
> > Of joy and grief, of pleasure and of pain.
>
> "Prolong" both takes meaning from the word "forms" and gives it. Because we have been partly persuaded that the forms of nature exist inwardly as well as outwardly, it makes literal sense to speak of the forms "prolonging" human feeling.[4]

The imaginative word in Wordsworth may, then, lie this side of metaphor, not, as one might have supposed, in the

[3] John Jones, *The Egotistical Sublime: A History of Wordsworth's Imagination* (London: Chatto & Windus, 1954), p. 85.
[4] Colin C. Clarke, *Romantic Paradox: an Essay on the Poetry of Wordsworth* (New York: Barnes & Noble, 1963), p. 26.

2

mystic reaches beyond metaphor, or in a realm of purely private associations.

Miss Josephine Miles and Geoffrey Hartman also discover unique features in Wordsworth's metaphoric practice. Miss Miles notes Wordsworth's dislike of glitter and suggests that a connection exists linking his dislike of glitter and his disuse of "glaring" metaphors; she concludes a brief discussion of the matter by stating that

> ... Wordsworth was referring in his criticisms not just to figures of speech or single words, but to the sum of these. A fault in perspective would lead, for Wordsworth, to a fault in metric, and a fault in vocabulary. The whole structure of falsity, from theme and attitude to single phrase, stood out in all its obviousness for Wordsworth in the frame of reality as he saw it; and he called elements in that structure "glaring," "glittering," and "glossy," with vigor and conviction.[5]

Wordsworth's rhetorical restraint may thus originate in the new epistemology and exhibit itself mainly in a few key words; but if it is, as Miss Miles indicates, a question of poetic structures and a pervasive attitude, we might be wrong not to look everywhere for evidence of a changed view of language. Hartman underscores Miss Miles's conclusion by pointing out that Wordsworth's poetry, at its best, is a "web of transfers," none of which is "showy or patently metaphorical"; he urges, moreover, that we approach the web with caution, out of deference not simply to Wordsworth's tastes but to his themes and the continuity of those larger narrative units whose transfers

[5] Josephine Miles, "Wordsworth and Glitter," in *Studies in Philology*, XL (1943), 559.

... indicate, in the presence of other signs, a dizzy openness of relation between the human mind and nature. Such to-and-fros ("traffickings") between inner and outer, literal and figurative, or present and past, often span entire episodes and even cross them.[6]

In the present study I attempt to approach the web. Volume II of the 1800 *Lyrical Ballads* seemed a logical focal point, for its poems are mature, yet stylistically experimental, and deserve more attention in this regard than they have received. I hope to answer specifically a question raised by Wordsworth's own quarrel with Gray's theory of poetic diction: the question of what, in practice, Wordsworth's alternative was. Abrams points the way to the present study in concluding that Wordsworth's chief concern

> ... is not with the single words or the grammatical order of prose discourse, but *with figurative departures from literal discourse*, and that Wordsworth's main intention is to show that such deviations are justifiable in verse only when they have the same psychological causes that they have in the "artless" speech of every day. Those who have thought to confound Wordsworth's argument by demonstrating that in his own poetry he uses a larger vocabulary and a different syntactic ordonnance than a peasant does, have largely missed the point.[7] [italics mine]

I agree with Abrams, but the question that remains to be answered is the question of how, in the poetry itself, Wordsworth introduces and controls those "figurative departures from literal discourse" without losing the

[6] Geoffrey H. Hartman, *Wordsworth's Poetry, 1787–1814* (New Haven: Yale University Press, 1964), p. 66.
[7] Abrams, *The Mirror and the Lamp*, p. 110.

naturalness and simplicity of everyday speech. The figures
that I discuss may not exhaust the list, but they provide, I
feel, a range sufficient to indicate not only that figurative
techniques may be profitably studied in Wordsworth, but
also that an examination of the poetry bears out Abrams'
suggestion of a relationship between Wordsworth's theory
of language and his poetic practice and that, in speaking of
poetry as consisting of "a selection of the language really
spoken by men,"[8] Wordsworth allows the poet some
discretion, apart from his use of meter, some poetic license,
in using those words and phrases derived from the language
of men in real life.

The figures I have isolated are those involving paradox
and equivocation, repetition, intransitive and transitive
predication, synecdoche, similitude and personification, and
metaphor. Paradox and equivocation are seen to be unique
in Wordsworth in that they provide a double view of their
subject, a view that enables Wordsworth to present his
subject as at once ordinary and unusual, in accordance with
the familiar statement of his purpose in the *Lyrical Ballads*:

> The principle object, then, proposed in these Poems was
> to choose incidents and situations from common life, and
> to relate or describe them, throughout, as far as was
> possible in a selection of language really used by men, and,
> at the same time, to throw over them a certain colouring of
> imagination, whereby ordinary things should be presented
> to the mind in an unusual aspect.[9]

[8] 1802 Preface, in E. de Selincourt and H. Darbishire (eds.), *The
Poetical Works of William Wordsworth* (5 vols.; Oxford: Clarendon
Press, 1940–1949), II, 392; hereafter referred to as *Poetical Works*;
Vol. II page references in my introduction only refer to Helen
Darbishire's 2nd ed. of Vol. II (Oxford: Clarendon Press, 1952).
[9] *Ibid.*, II, 386.

5

Wordsworth goes on to say that he is interested "above all" in tracing in his descriptions "the primary laws of our nature." Here already the two limiting terms affecting all of Wordsworth's figurative language, as shall be indicated later—the mind and external nature—appear just beneath the surface, in the shift from "common life" to "our nature." Paradox and equivocation tend to bind the two terms inextricably in the poem.

The simile in Wordsworth, which is seen to be closely connected with his technique of concrete personification, is also unique in that it is his means of distributing or diffusing human characteristics throughout nature and of thereby linking person and place, in accordance with his aim expressed elsewhere of making his poetry conversant with truth "not individual and local, but general, and operative."[10] By using the simile to link person and place, Wordsworth manages to present "the passions of men . . . incorporated with the beautiful and permanent forms of nature."[11] For Wordsworth, place apparently *is* the "general and operative" principle in his formulation, and, by relating person to place through the simile, Wordsworth succeeds in universalizing character poetically.

The remaining figures—figures involving repetition, predication, synecdoche, and metaphor—all function in ways similar to those of paradox, equivocation, and similitude, in that they, too, serve toward the general end of verbally "approximating" man and nature and of rendering possible a poetic account of the special kind of intercourse between man and nature that Wordsworth is nearly everywhere concerned with recording. Repetition in

[10] *Ibid.*, II, 394.
[11] *Ibid.*, II, 387.

Wordsworth is not only a means of expressing passion; it is also a means of bringing the actual and the ideal, the literal and the symbolic, into close relation. The raising of the actual to the ideal is in Wordsworth a function of time and memory, in conjunction with a guiding spirit within nature; poetic repetition of the sort discussed here is an extension of the natural process, as Wordsworth sees it, beyond life and into art. The verb structures and synecdoches discussed here assist Wordsworth in dramatizing the encounter and rapprochement of mind and nature, the signal "actions" of Wordsworth's spousal verse. The metaphor in Wordsworth is seen to be unique, not only in that it is subdued and structurally introduced, but also in that it everywhere draws us into Wordsworth's cosmology by drawing consistently upon, and by erasing the ordinary distinctions between, the animate and inanimate realms.

Personification is given separate consideration here, yet it tends to be a function of several figures and not a figure in its own right. As is true of several of the figures examined here, personification is as much the matter as the manner of the poem in which it is introduced, and in this respect it illustrates the problem taken up in the conclusion of this study—the problem of separating manner from matter in Wordsworth. Concerning repetition of the expressive sort, and poetic language in general, Wordsworth has this to say:

> There are also various other reasons why repetition and apparent tautology are frequently beauties of the highest kind. Among the chief of these reasons is the interest which the mind attaches to words, not only as symbols of the passion, but as *things*, active and efficient, which are of themselves part of the passion.[12]

[12] 1800 note to "The Thorn," in *ibid.*, II, 513.

On one level this argument may perhaps best be understood as a summary of Wordsworth's entire argument against the theory of poetic diction that had given rise to the use of a "motley masquerade of tricks, quaintnesses, hieroglyphics, and enigmas"[13] in the worst poetry of his own and earlier eras. It is not the use of figurative language in itself to which Wordsworth objects, but the divorce of figurative language from the feeling that did once and should always alone give rise to such language. In this, Wordsworth continues the argument with which Hugh Blair prefaces his discussion of tropes and figures:

> The fact is [writes Blair], that the strongly pathetic, and the pure sublime, not only have little dependance on figures of speech, but, generally, reject them. The proper region of these ornaments is, where a moderate degree of elevation and passion is predominant; and there they contribute to the embellishment of discourse, only, when there is a basis of solid thought and natural sentiment; when they are inserted in their proper place; and when they rise, of themselves, from the subject, without being sought after.[14]

Wordsworth of course extends the argument by defining poetry *as* passion ("the Reader cannot be too often reminded that Poetry is passion")[15] and by defining figurative language as, in true poetry, extraordinary passion ("feeling powerfully as they [the earliest poets] did, their language was daring, and figurative").[16]

Perhaps too much effort has been expended in attempts

[13] Appendix on Poetic Diction, in *ibid.*, II, 406.
[14] Hugh Blair, *Lectures on Rhetoric and Belles Lettres* (2 vols.; London, 1783), I, 279 (lecture xiv).
[15] 1800 note to "The Thorn," in *Poetical Works*, II, 513.
[16] Appendix on Poetic Diction, in *ibid.*, II, 405.

to understand Wordsworth's critical utterances by studying those utterances in isolation from his poetry. The trouble with Wordsworth's deliverances in his prefaces, in the words of Abrams, who echoes Coleridge, is that they are "peculiarly dark and equivocal." [17] Moreover, Hartman offers us this reminder:

> Wordsworth's theory of words, except for the significant attack on poetic diction, took the form of poetry rather than prose, and is more reticent than in Coleridge, Hopkins, or the modern poet. But his unique style, in which metaphor (transference) is a generalized structure rather than a special verbal figure, though I have tried to describe it, remains unexplored in its larger implications.[18]

My method is accordingly that of exploring several of the representative earlier poems from the standpoint of the effects of the recurring figures indicated earlier and of presenting the relationships I find between those figures and the main themes of their respective poems. My findings will naturally be restricted by my scope, for there are many features of the poems I discuss which I must forego comment on if I am to accomplish my aim with reasonable brevity. I must even pass reluctantly over matters that have in the past concerned critical readers of the poems taken up here. I can only point out that I have made every effort to avoid giving partial readings of the poems—every effort, that is, short of what I feared might tempt me too far afield. A few figures, then, and some major themes, and their implications as far as Wordsworth's theory of language is concerned, are the subject of the present study.

[17] Abrams, *The Mirror and the Lamp*, p. 110.
[18] Hartman, *Wordsworth's Poetry*, p. xi.

9

In a positive way, what I hope to offer are readings that demonstrate to some degree how delicately Wordsworth's language responds at the level of grammar and diction to the pulse of feeling that rolls through some of his best poetry, how his themes, his "passions," give shape to, or are shaped by, his language. The interminglings of theme and figure are finally, it appears to me, translations into the language of poetry of that ennobling interchange between mind and nature chronicled in *The Prelude* (as well as translated there, too). In this final unity of life and art is poetry truly "the image of man and nature"[19] and "the breath and finer spirit of all knowledge."[20]

[19] 1800 Preface, in *Poetical Works*, II, 395.
[20] *Ibid.*, II, 396.

I

Paradox and Equivocation

Every student of the English Romantic poets knows that Wordsworth's task in the *Lyrical Ballads* was "to give the charm of novelty to things of every day," as Coleridge puts it,[1] and he also knows of Wordsworth's predilection for exact description.[2] Cleanth Brooks is one of the few critics since Coleridge who have explored in any detail, however, the matter of how Wordsworth pressed beyond the descriptive exactitude he cherished and attained a novelty that precise description alone cannot be depended on to supply.[3] Because of the gentleness with which Wordsworth shocks us out of our habitual ways of seeing things, it is certainly possible to take many of his images not for what they are, but for earnest efforts at exact description. The

[1] S. T. Coleridge, *Biographia Literaria, with his Aesthetical Essays* ed. J. Shawcross (2 vols.; Oxford: Clarendon Press, 1907), II, 6.

[2] See "Essay, Supplementary to the Preface" (1815), in *Poetical Works*, II, 423; "... I have felt," writes Wordsworth, "the falsehood that pervades the volumes imposed upon the world under the name of Ossian. From what I saw with my own eyes, I knew that the imagery was spurious. In nature everything is distinct, yet nothing defined into absolute independent singleness."

[3] Cleanth Brooks, *The Well Wrought Urn: Studies in the Structure of Poetry* (New York: Reynal & Hitchcock, 1947), pp. 3–7.

secret of such images, however, where they succeed, is not in their exact description, but in the way they evince a "charm of novelty," as in the lines

> With many a wanton stroke
> Her feet disperse the powd'ry snow
> That rises up like smoke.
>
> ("Lucy Gray," ll. 26–28)[4]

Wordsworth's careful glance tells him that under certain circumstances the eye might for a fleeting moment take snow to be smoke; one senses that were this not possible, he would reject the image. But its value in the poem clearly hinges on the likelihood that under ordinary circumstances no careful observer of nature would confuse the two, for it is the extraordinary quality of the snow, thus likened to smoke, that gives rise to our sense of nature's participation in Lucy Gray's blithe and wanton mood. The image seems, upon reflection, less a created than a discovered paradox, one that has been come upon by accident and then exploited for thematic purposes, and not one simply invented for effect. The exactness of the description lends it a quality of "truth to nature"; its force, however, is in the applicability of its suggestion of life-in-death to Lucy's circumstances (the snow, which is dead, "rises up," anticipating the broad transformation that Lucy undergoes in the poem from being a real but misled bearer of light, to being a legendary figure in the neighborhood, an effectual bearer of light, a [truly] "living child").

[4] The text used for the poems of 1800 is William Wordsworth and S. T. Coleridge, *Lyrical Ballads, 1798 and 1800*, ed. R. L. Brett and A. R. Jones (New York: Barnes & Noble, 1963).

Wordsworth's use of visual paradox, of momentary illusion, can be observed even more closely in the following passage, which introduces, in place of a simile, the sharper novelty of a more overt personification:

> The hare is running races in her mirth;
> And with her feet she from the plashy earth
> Raises a mist; that, glittering in the sun,
> Runs with her all the way, wherever she doth run.
> ("Resolution and Independence," ll. 11–14)

Again he appears to discover rather than invent his paradox, though in this case he heightens it through a double use of the verb "runs," which is, one will notice, a personifying verb so idiomatic and timeworn as to have become literal. Wordsworth revitalizes it in his application of it to his exactly rendered anomaly, once in connection with the hare (an animate thing) and once in connection with the mist (an inanimate thing). The first "runs" borrows some of its force from the second, that of the hare, and thus heightens our sense that the mist is something alive and volitional. The hare, like the poet in his youth or in the meadow (the ascent in the poem is a progress-through-life metaphor), is the unwitting or blind recipient of nature's blessings (hence the strong personification of the double "runs"), visual blessings which the aging poet now sees, but no longer enjoys; higher up yet, where he encounters the leech-gatherer, however, he will receive a more valuable gift, an eloquent apparition of Independent Man, a gift offered to him not through a visual, but through an auditory anomaly (the illusion that the old man's voice is the voice of the waters, a voice that echoes down to us from the creation).

13

Another type of surface paradox frequently to be encountered in Wordsworth is what might be called the inappropriate modifier. While it is less dramatic than the figures based on anomalies of appearance, Wordsworth uses it more often, and it therefore brings us closer to the verbal texture of his poetry. Three instances of this figure are underlined in the following excerpts from "It Was an April morning":

> ... the voice
> Of waters which the winter had supplied
> Was soften'd down into a *vernal tone*.

> ... beast and bird, the lamb,
> The Shepherd's dog, the linnet and the thrush
> Vied with this waterfall, and made a song
> Which, while I listen'd seem'd like the wild growth
> Or like some natural *produce of the air*
> That could not cease to be. Green leaves were here,
> But 'twas the *foliage of the rocks*, the birch,
> The yew, the holly, and the bright green thorn,
> With hanging islands of resplendent furze.

> (ll. 3–5 and 25–33)

The three modifiers are "vernal," "of the air," and "of the rocks." "Vernal" refers of course to spring and to foliation, but what a "vernal tone" is, the reader must infer from his own experience of hearing the sound of water in the spring, or when it is muffled by surrounding growth. The "appropriate" verbalization of the idea would be "the sound of water in the spring"; the expression "vernal tone," with its crossover between the visual and the auditory, strikes the modern reader especially as much to be preferred, for we tend to be highly tolerant of all means of poetic compression. In this tolerance, however, we are at somewhat of a dis-

14

advantage in reading Wordsworth, for only if the figure "vernal tone" stands out for us does it serve to prefigure the two other crossovers cited above, and only in the latter event does it support the poem's theme of continual change as opposed to abrupt cessation. The term "vernal" has a wide currency in the nature poetry of the eighteenth century, but Wordsworth's application of it is novel; thus, while it must have rung familiar to his immediate audience, its *use* must have seemed strange. Here, as in all his figurative usages, it is the slightly off-key element that he exploits.

That strangeness is still fresh for us in the lines "like the wild growth / Or like some natural produce of the air," both because it is an unusual comparison, even to our jaded ears, and because its diction is less dated than that of the first crossover. We can thus perhaps gauge more accurately its probable effect on Wordsworth's contemporaries, for whom it must have seemed striking, conveying as it does even to us a sense of the quietly fantastic. The effect is muffled somewhat by Wordsworth's use of a simile instead of a metaphor, but it is deepened by the earlier "vernal tone," which involves the same terms, the same harmony of opposites. The poem as a whole affords a clear picture of how Wordsworth went about assimilating the strange and at the same time sharpening the familiar. For a contrasting method, one could turn to Yeats's poem "A Coat,"[5] in which Yeats, introducing a wide rupture between his tenor and his vehicle, builds upon a comparison of song or poem and coat and achieves his purpose with a much imitated mixture of defiance and bathos. That he drew his metaphoric technique directly or indirectly from Byron suggests

[5] W. B. Yeats, *Collected Poems* (New York: Macmillan, 1951), p. 125.

that the unifying principle in the poem is the self, not the external world, and that its metaphor dramatizes an ironic awareness, an apartness from nature, not a discovered affinity between human nature and the external world. Wordsworth appropriately closes the rupture in his comparison by only briefly describing an audible fact as though it were a visual fact and then quickly retreating into the literal. Yet he never lets go of the correspondences he reveals.

The last and possibly the most subtle inappropriate modifier of the group—the phrase "of the rocks" in "foliage of the rocks"—would pass for straight literal usage were it not for the motif of permanence in the passage where it occurs. It has a fairly strong literal sense, namely that the plants referred to as "foliage" are all indigenous to their rocky terrain. We are told, however, that the rocky glen in which they are come upon is a "continuous" glen (line 21), and that the sounds Wordsworth hears there seem to him a song "that could not cease to be" (line 30). In this context, the phrase "foliage of the rocks" suggests, at least momentarily, that the foliage is either made from rock and thus cannot wither, or that it is in some other way miraculously permanent. The immutability that one discovers in connection with these natural objects remains associated with the objects, yet the quality is all the while appropriate not to them, but to the *image* of the place as it exists in Wordsworth's mind; the dell is one of those places so beautiful that if one were but to spend some time there—

> He would so love it that in his death-hour
> Its image would survive among his thoughts.
> ("To M. H.")

In what I have called the "inappropriate" modifier, one begins to notice a tipping of the scales with regard to the "conferred" as distinct from "inherent" values Wordsworth speaks of in the 1815 Preface, a moving toward "conferred" values. That is, in creating such images as "foliage of the rocks," Wordsworth did not so much abstract from objects "some of those [properties] which [they] actually possess" as "confer additional properties" upon them.[6] The Intimations Ode contains several "inappropriate" or "conferred" modifiers, notably "fields of sleep" (line 28), "a place of thought" (line 124), and "the being of the eternal Silence" (lines 159–160). Each phrase functions in a unique way, depending upon its content and context, but all of them involve unexpected shifts from one realm of experience to another; by slightly disordering our vision, they bring us close to the central concerns of their respective poems.

The equivocal term in Wordsworth does not always at first strike one as being equivocal, because he takes great care in most instances to keep his expression closely literal on at least one plane of meaning. However, in the ostensibly descriptive poem "To Joanna," the expression "the living stone" (line 83) emerges finally as more than just descriptive. The word "living" in this instance has a literal meaning, if one takes it as denoting a quality lent to the rock by its "intermixture of delicious hues" (line 47), hues supplied by the shrubs, trees, and flowers that grow on its face; in this reading, "living stone" involves merely a harmless compression. Yet is it, in context, really harmless, really literal? Or does it not echo lines 54–55?

[6] 1815 Preface, in *Poetical Works*, II, 438.

> The rock, like something starting from a sleep
> Took up the Lady's voice, and laughed again.

In terms of the broader structure of the poem, the description of the rock's "delicious hues" might be thought to advance the notion of a visual, "self-connecting" life early in the poem, if one takes the word "life" in the sense of "vivid" and therefore "animated." Then, of course, the rock springs to life in Wordsworth's fancy (lines 54–55), and is finally called a "living stone" in the later and more declarative, settled passage which appears to affirm the argument of the opening of the poem that one may "look upon the hills with tenderness, / And make dear friendships with the streams and groves" (lines 7–8).

In other instances of such terms, one's immediate reaction to the term may be, not that it is equivocal, but that it is simply supererogatory. A few such terms are italicized in the following lines from "Michael":

> I will relate the same
> For the delight of a few *natural* hearts.   (ll. 35–36)

> Fields, where with chearful spirits he had breath'd
> The *common* air.   (ll. 65–66)

> thou hast been bound to me
> Only by *links* of love.   (ll. 411–412)

It might be argued that only the first of these terms, "natural," is equivocal, and yet they all raise questions, if not regarding their meaning, then regarding the reason for their inclusion in passages that make quite good sense without them. "Common" and "natural" are terms that

Wordsworth seems to have a special fondness for, and both can take surprising turns in meaning. Their ostensible meanings (and we are seldom quite without an ostensible meaning in Wordsworth) are, in the case of "natural," free of debasing influences or soul-destroying restraints, and, for "common," ordinary or everyday. In spite of their acceptability in context given these meanings, they seem to beg some deeper meaning, for with only their ordinary meanings they add very little to the sense of their passages— too little, really, to justify their presence. The term "natural" would prove too involved for use as an example here, because of the historical concepts of nature it opens onto; yet what holds true for "common" in this connection holds true for "natural" as well.

The word "common" in "Michael" should lead us quickly from the thought of something ordinary to the thought of something shared, and ultimately to the poem's theme of love. In the course of the poem, we see Michael's love drawn from the hills and fields and redirected toward Luke, at first that in Luke which seems most to epitomize nature— Luke's cheeks, described as "two steady roses," and those emanations from Luke described as "light to the sun and music to the wind" (line 212). One is tempted to view these manifestations of Michael's affection for Luke as merely expressive figurative heightenings justified by his passion, which of course they are; but the images do more: if we had not sensed it in Michael's wish to have the sheepfold be a covenant and memorial linking Luke and himself, we sense here that Michael needs outward support for his love, that he stands in need of the mediation of natural objects or images in order to love any other human being, even his own son, throughout most of the poem. The quality of his relationship with Luke is of course more fluid than can be indicated here, for there is also implicitly a sense in which Michael's love of nature depends upon his love for Luke ("Why should I relate / That objects which the Shepherd loved before / Were dearer now?" [lines 208–210]). The mere fact, however, that the air is called "common," this time in the sense of communal or shared, indicates in just one small way the kind of nurture Michael had received from the hills and fields, for he had observed the principle of sharing, the "common" qualities, in all the objects of nature that had surrounded him. Michael's love for Luke is a love shared by Luke and nature, and in that it tends to shift from nature to Luke, Luke has nature to thank for Michael's kind feelings toward him, bound up as Michael's affections are with nature.

Closely related to the ideas that the word "common" touches upon is the word "blind," which is used to describe Michael's feeling toward nature and, later, his feeling toward Luke as well. We first meet it in lines 74–79, in which Wordsworth summarizes Michael's relationship with nature at the opening of the poem:

> these fields, these hills
> Which were his living Being, even more
> Than his own Blood—what could they less? had laid
> Strong hold on his affections, were to him
> A pleasurable feeling of blind love,
> The pleasure which there is in life itself.

The next time we meet it is in lines 149–153, in which Wordsworth summarizes Michael's relationship with *Luke*:

20

> but to Michael's heart
> This Son of his old age was yet more dear—
> Effect which might perhaps have been produc'd
> By that instinctive tenderness, the same
> Blind Spirit, which is in the blood of all.

The term "Blind Spirit" may be read as "instinct," but the recurrence both of "blind" and "blood" makes the echo clear and affirms that Michael's love for Luke is indeed the same love he had felt for nature, transferred to Luke. The "common" or shared quality of Michael's love is thus prefigured by the phrase "the common air" and by the image of the hills that "link" his acts of kindness to his certainty of gain. The mere word "common" conveys in itself little of all this, and yet once one grasps and reflects upon the broad theme of "Michael," subsequent readings tell one how few such word choices in Wordsworth are based on circumstantial considerations.

What has been said so far about the theme of love in "Michael" may have made it already plain what function is performed by the initially puzzling expression "links of love," for if natural objects (and in Wordsworth certain man-made objects blessed by time and the elements may be called such) mediate between man and man, then natural objects may be called literally "links of love." The sheepfold is one such link; through it the power of nature works quietly to join Michael and Luke and gives promise of an enduring quality in their love that will enable it to outlast separation, and perhaps death itself. The principle of mediation involved here is no different from that whereby nature is said at the outset of the poem to have led Wordsworth to esteem the dwellers in the valleys,

men
Whom I already lov'd, not verily
For their own sakes, but for the fields and hills
Where was their occupation and abode.   (ll. 23–26)

Human love thus appears to originate from, and to be reposited in, natural objects. In a sense, such objects, considered as "links," may be thought of not as repositories of love in a merely figurative way, but in a literal way as well. That Dorothy considered the heartlike shape of the sheepfold worth noting[7] suggests a habit of free identification that would allow for a considering of the stones as a kind of corporeal residuum or condensation of love.

Thus, once more, the single word that at first glance seems hardly necessary, upon further consideration offers the reader a choice of whether to take it literally or figuratively; and the making of a choice, the penetration of the questions it raises, often entails the making of a choice as to the meaning of the entire experience it forms a part of, and ultimately of course the meaning of the entire poem.

The present discussion has deviated somewhat from the subject of style in the limited sense, but only to demonstrate that in Wordsworth style is deeply rooted in the theme and substance of the poem. That Wordsworth very seldom puns, but very often equivocates in such a way as to lead us up to a place from which we can discern the common vanishing point of two experiences, provides elementary evidence of the deep bond in Wordsworth between the word and the quality of the experience it records. To use the term "ambiguity" instead of the unfortunately pejorative term "equivocation" would only obscure an important fact:

[7] See Dorothy's journal entry in the note on "Michael," in *ibid.*, II, 479; see also William's comments on the poem in the same note.

Wordsworth characteristically imposes rather strict limitations on his language through his contexts; his themes are profound, but few, and when we cast about for "chance" networks of meaning, we meet, coming and going, the same themes. The magic alternatives of the Wordsworthian term appear to be to explore, on the one hand, its ties with the realm of literal and scrupulous fact, and, on the other hand, its ties with a realm in which the soul of man and the soul of nature commune.[8] The key words, like his key natural objects, are media that communicate between these realms and acquire their fullest significance for us only when examined in the light of both. The initial difficulty with Wordsworth's paradoxes, in particular, is that they can seldom be verified or construed on both of their planes of meaning by pointing to an incontrovertible structure of events or meanings, as in the allegory; this difficulty is attested to by long disputes such as that over the phrase "fields of sleep."[9] The only way in which such problems of interpretation are finally to be resolved, in the absence of conclusive evidence, is through a broad knowledge of Wordsworth's themes and a habit of letting each word and phrase work on us "like a new existence."[10]

[8] See Émile Legouis, *The Early Life of William Wordsworth, 1770–1798*, trans. J W. Matthews (London: J. W. Dent & Sons, 1921), p. 454: "Every sensation," writes Legouis, "ought to bring us, and actually does bring us, into touch, not with the object which gives it birth, but with the soul which that object conceals,—with absolute truth. It is a dialogue between the *soul* of man and the *soul* of external things."

[9] See J. V. Logan, *Wordsworthian Criticism: A Guide and Bibliography* (Columbus, Ohio: Ohio State University Press, 1947), entries 69 and 270; and E. F. Henley and D. H. Stam (comps.), *Wordsworthian Criticism, 1945–1959: An Annotated Bibliography* (New York: New York Public Library, 1960), entries 26 and 304.

[10] 1815 Preface, in *Poetical Works*, II, 438.

23

2

Three Experiments in Word-Repetition

"Tintern Abbey" is chiefly concerned with a change in the quality of Wordsworth's love of nature, a change that might be most briefly described as a passing beyond the love of sensation into the love of thought. How to convey the idea that thought itself is something he gains from nature is the problem that the poem must have presented to Wordsworth. He solves it by suggesting that what he now (in the poem) sees in nature is at once broader in range and yet simpler, purer, and more inward (more deeply felt, if still perceived without) than the merely visual attractions that had earlier drawn him to nature. Nature, he says, has become for him music, motion, and spirit, rather than simply color and shape. Perhaps his full discussion should be included here, even though it is perhaps the best-known passage in Wordsworth:

> I cannot paint
> What then I was. The sounding cataract
> Haunted me like a passion: the tall rock,
> The mountains, and the deep and gloomy wood,
> Their colours and their forms, were then to me
> An appetite: a feeling and a love,

That had no need of a remoter charm,
By thought supplied, or any interest
Unborrowed from the eye.

    . . . . . .

                   I have learned
To look on nature, not as in the hour
Of thoughtless youth, but hearing oftentimes
The still, sad music of humanity,
Not harsh nor grating, though of ample power
To chasten and subdue. And I have felt
A presence that disturbs me with the joy
Of elevated thoughts; a sense sublime
Of something far more deeply interfused,
Whose dwelling is the light of setting suns,
And the round ocean, and the living air,
And the blue sky, and in the mind of man,
A motion and a spirit, that impels
All thinking things, all objects of all thought,
And rolls through all things. Therefore am I still
 A lover of the meadows and the woods,
And mountains; and of all that we behold
From this green earth.   (ll. 76–84 and 89–106)

Color itself has almost ceased to be a sensation; there are
no more "aching joys" or "dizzy raptures" of color and
form, there is just the blue sky and "this green earth." The
purification of color, introduced as an aspect of the life of
thought, becomes our primary clue as to the quality of the
opening landscape (lines 1–23) that makes it, of all possible
landscapes, the one best suited to provide outward con-
firmation of Wordsworth's inward, moral change, and
worthy to open such a poem. Its harmony and simplicity
are in its interwoven foliage and its greenness. The following
passage not only explicitly introduces the losing of form

within form, but also repeats the word "green" three times:

> these orchard-tufts,
> Which, at this season, with their unripe fruits,
> Among the woods and copses lose themselves,
> Nor, with their green and simple hue, disturb
> The wild green landscape. Once again I see
> These hedge-rows, hardly hedge-rows, little lines
> Of sportive wood run wild; these pastoral farms
> Green to the very door. (ll. 11–18)

Lines 1–23 contain a still subtler form of repetition, not of the whole word "green," but of the sounds it is comprised of. All sounds recur, of course, with great frequency, but the frequency indicated in the list below gives these twenty-three lines a consonance which, if it were alliterative, one would all too quickly hear. Simply reading through the list of words, none of which appears twice on the list, will give some idea of how the word "green" is kept as it were phonemically alive, how it is emphasized and "interfused" through a kind of physical distribution of the word:[1]

[1] An analogous passage in Andrew Marvell's "The Garden," lines 41–48 (I am indebted to Donald C. Bryant for pointing out the passage), exhibits a similar distribution of "ē" and "n," though not of other sounds related to the word "green." Many another analogous passage of poetry undoubtedly exists, but symbolic heightening by such means of distribution, as distinct from occasional reinforcement of sense through sound by the use of alliteration or assonance, does not seem to be the practice in Augustan poetry, nor is it in the earlier Wordsworth. In "The Female Vagrant," lines 208–225, for example, where memory and the sensations following upon separation from nature are treated and where one would look for such heightening, we find no such repetition. A check of random passages in Wordsworth and elsewhere convinces me of the statistical significance of the present table of sounds in lines 1–23 of "Tintern Abbey."

Word	Line		Word	Line
Sound			*Sound*	
"gn"			**"ē"**	
again	2		these	3
again	4		sweet	4
again	9		these	5
again	14		steep	5
			deep	7
			these	11
"rn"–"nr"			these	11
unripe	12		see	15
run	17		these	16
			these	17
			seem	20
"grn"				
ground	11		**sustained "n"**	
vagrant	21		mountain	3
			inland	4
			seclusion	7
"grēn"			and	7
green	14		landscape	8
green	15		lines	16
green	18		uncertain	20
			alone	23
"rē"				
wreathes	18			
trees	19			
"ēn"				
scene	6			
season	12			

28

Other words such as "years," "hear," "summer," and "murmur" set up closely related resonances that help to extend the "green" into almost every half-line of the passage. If it is possible to repeat a word by so distributing its sounds and making them the dominant sounds of a passage, then it is true of these lines, for in few comparable passages does one find a restricted set of sounds so pervasively present. The objection might be raised that the word "green" is not what is distributed, but some other word, for example "again." "Again" is a very important word here and does in fact share in the distribution; it is important because it emphasizes that a past time is being revived. But it is not the most important word, for it must be remembered that the greenness is visually, and therefore more immediately, dominant in the scene or image and that it is reinforced twice again in the poem, once in the lines

> Therefore am I still
> A lover of the meadows and the woods,
> And mountains, and of all that we behold
> From this green earth   (ll. 103–106)

and once at the end of the poem.

In terms of the poem as a whole, the green of the opening landscape becomes the correlative of Wordsworth's accession to the life of thought, it becomes the element of thought—tranquillity—in nature, and, finally, it becomes a symbol. The term "symbol" did not then have the currency it now has; the term "ideal," rather than symbolic, would perhaps be more apt, historically speaking, though our term symbolic conveys a somewhat closer notion of the character of the image to us. The quality of depth of idea noticeable in "green," its symbolic quality, would seem to be the quality in Wordsworth's language that Coleridge is attempting to explain in his well-known summary of the Wordsworthian style; his meaning would probably be clearer for us had he used the term "symbolic" where we find him using "ideal":

> [Wordsworth's poetry exemplifies] the union of deep feeling with profound thought; the fine balance of truth in observing, with the imaginative faculty in modifying the objects observed; and above all the original gift of spreading the tone, the *atmosphere*, and with it the depth and height of the ideal world around forms, incidents, and situations, of which, for the common view, custom had bedimmed all the lustre, had dried up the sparkle and the dew drops.[2]

"Tintern Abbey" gives to "this green earth" a height and depth of idea by establishing the color green as the outward counterpart of the moral regeneration of the speaker. Through its contrast with the dizzy raptures of color and form in youth, and through subtle repetitions, green tends to emerge as the external manifestation of an inwardly felt harmony, as the "idea" of harmony, of thought itself, in nature. It is the greenness of nature that is "deeply interfused," and that impresses his mind with "a sense sublime / Of something far more deeply interfused" (lines 96–97). His former state is refracted in the shooting lights of Dorothy's wild eyes, but his present state is reflected by the subdued greens, the "quietness and beauty" (line 127) of the nature before him. His moral recognition is not merely that he has lost the aching joys of youth; it is that his new condition has placed him in harmony with nature once

[2] *Biographia Literaria*, I, 59.

again, but this time in its higher mood, and that separation has not resulted in alienation from nature. There is further satisfaction in finding that he can, almost at will, symbolically transmit the "sober pleasure" he has discovered both within and without (lines 1–23 *are* the discovery, the germ of the poem) in the form of poetry, for if the germ of the poem is half-created and half-perceived, it would not have sufficed that his memory had been a dwelling place for his symbols. He had to return to nature, as in life he returned to Dorothy; the pure memories, pure abstractions, needed present objects in order for him to be able to form *poetic* symbols.

The incomplete comparison of "far more deeply interfused" (line 97) may be strategically incomplete, for it drives us back across the poem, much as the "soft inland murmurs" reverse the seaward movement of the waters. Almost any, or all, of the several interfusions of the poem might be intended; there are the green hues that lose themselves in one another, the overlapping of past and present images of the landscape, his own youthful pleasure reflected in Dorothy's eyes, and perhaps other interfusions still. Surely that which is far *more* deeply interfused, however, is man and nature, more deeply now because they are bound spiritually, in thought, not in sensation. The most important contrast in the poem is the contrast of the "glad animal" boy and the solitary Hermit. Both are in harmony (are interfused) with nature, the boy with its aching joys (sensations), the Hermit with its green and sober pleasures (the "spirit, that impels / All thinking things, all objects of all thought" [lines 100–101]). Green is, finally, the poem's overriding symbol of the latter, the present condition or union of man and nature, and the poem's multiple harmonies come to rest in a green image:

31

> Nor wilt thou then forget,
> That after many wanderings, many years
> Of absence, these steep woods and lofty cliffs,
> And this green pastoral landscape, were to me
> More dear, both for themselves and for thy sake!
>
> (ll. 156–160)

The next experiment in repetition brings us to the poetry of the Goslar period. In the "Lucy" poems and in "Ruth," the notion of a crossing over from the life in sensation to the life in thought is correlated with a series of poetic dream-waking sequences. The dreaming is not dreaming in the ordinary sense, however, but is a paradoxical dreaming-with-open-eyes:

> In one of those sweet dreams I slept,
> Kind Nature's gentlest boon!
> And all the while my eyes I kept
> On the descending moon.
>
> ("Strange fits of passion," ll. 17–20)

In all of the relevant poems, the action flows uninterruptedly through dream and waking states, though the quality of awareness changes; the "dreaming" is metaphoric for illusion and does not imply the cessation of conscious activity or the interruption of sensation. If it implies anything, "dreaming" implies a total preoccupation with sensation, a slumber of the spirit prolonged by an all too wakeful eye.

The dream-waking sequence supplies "Ruth" with a submerged structure. That is, the poem opens with a green, "waking" landscape in England; Ruth's attention, however, soon shifts from England to America, a place which in its various colors may be taken as a "dream" landscape, and the imagery does not reflect her return in thought to her green, "waking" England until her young man abandons her and she recovers from her bout with madness. This structure makes possible a kind of repetition that differs from the simple principle of reiteration we found in "Tintern Abbey," for here repetition is reduced to two important occurrences of each term, one in a "waking" portion of the poem and one in a "dream" portion of the poem. This underlying structure provides the necessary modification and renders one instance of each term symbolic or ideal.

Three terms in particular undergo in "Ruth" a slight disordering or "idealization" as a result of being thus repeated; they are "father," "bower," and "home." Several other words are repeated in much the same manner, but these are perhaps the clearest instances of idealization, the most substantive examples. Ruth's father is introduced at the opening of the poem, before the onset of Ruth's "dream," her turning in imagination to nature; he is in fact the cause of her turning wholly and disastrously to nature, for he is said to have slighted Ruth for his new mate:

> When Ruth was left half desolate,
> Her father took another Mate;
> And so, not seven years old,
> The slighted Child at her own will
> Went wandering over dale and hill
> In thoughtless freedom bold. (ll. 1–6)

Ruth's physical naturalization is suggested by her pipe of straw and her building of a bower:

> And she had made a pipe of straw
> And from that oaten pipe could draw
> All sounds of winds and floods;

33

Had built a bower upon the green,
As if she from her birth had been
An infant of the woods.   (ll. 7–12)

The fact that her bower is "on the green" suggests that as
yet her naturalization is only physical, and not imaginative
or total. The latter is marked by the sudden shift in the
imagery in stanza iii from the simple green and the sounds
of winds and floods to the varied splendors of the exotic
youth from America, whose appearance is as sudden and
unaccountable, one might say, as the free imagination could
wish:

There came a Youth from Georgia's shore,
A military Casque he wore
With splendid feathers drest;.
He brought them from the Cherokees;
The feathers nodded in the breeze
And made a gallant crest.   (ll. 13–18)

The very nodding of his feathers suggests the onset of a
trance or dream, in the sense of a total transfixion by
sensation, a total naturalization of Ruth's imagination.

In her "dream," the words "father" and "bower"
reappear imaginatively augmented through their association
with America:

And then he sometimes interwove
Dear thoughts about a Father's love,
"For there," said he, "are spun
Around the heart such tender ties
That our own children to our eyes
Are dearer than the sun.   (ll. 79–84)

34

This father is everything that Ruth's father is not, but his poetic significance for us lies less in his quality suggestive of a wish fulfillment on Ruth's part, though this factor is important, than in his relationship to a whole world, "A banner bright that was unfurled / Before me suddenly" (1805, lines 68–69). Overwhelmed by the beauty of that world, Ruth marries the young man who paints it for her, at which point the narrative is punctuated by the ominous reminder—"Through dream and vision did she sink" (line 103). The other side of the bright banner, its danger to Ruth's spiritual being, is soon introduced again with the reappearance of the bower in Ruth's dream-landscape:

> Nor less to feed voluptuous thought
> The beauteous forms of Nature wrought,
> Fair trees and lovely flowers;
> The breezes their own langour lent,
> The stars had feelings which they sent
> Into those magic bowers.   (ll. 127–132)

"Voluptuous," we soon see, is another alert to moral danger. The word "lawful" creeps into Ruth's thoughts as a kind of dream-censor that contends with "voluptuous," but it loses out to the latter, to lawlessness, upon the young man's defection, his becoming "As lawless as before" (line 162).

The word "home" in a way counterbalances the word "bower," for it first appears not at the opening but at the height of the dream portion of the poem, and then again, in a new modulation, in the depiction of the green landscape in the last part of the poem. Its use suggests that the concept of home is engendered by the very vision that stands as a threat to Ruth's spiritual existence. The mixed blessings of the life in sensation are seldom in Wordsworth gathered into so short a poem. The first mention of the word home occurs in the following context, and is "ideal":

> "How sweet it were
> A fisher or a hunter there,
> A gardener in the shade,
> Still wandering with an easy mind
> To build a household fire and find
> A home in every glade."   (ll. 67–72)

The waking repetition of the word brings with it a sense of something lost and lends a poignancy to Ruth's later pathetic situation:

> A barn her *winter* bed supplies,
> But till the warmth of summer skies
> And summer days is gone,
> (And in this tale we all agree)
> She sleeps beneath the greenwood tree,
> And other home hath none.   (ll. 199–204)

The waking fact is usually a paradox: just as nature in Wordsworth is never quite adequate to youthful yearning, though nature itself gives rise to that yearning with its vivid sensations, so Ruth's home is a home, and yet not a home, or at least not the home nature had seemed to paint for her; a new, green nature (the old nature seen through the eyes of experience) leads Ruth beyond "dream and vision." The dream fact, in this case the idealized home in America, is usually a fulfillment but also a peril to the soul; the soul must be led beyond, led back to the actual. In abandoning Ruth, her young husband functions as a stand-in for nature (he is the epitome of sensory or illusory nature); he accomplishes for Ruth her necessary awakening from the slumber that had sealed her spirit.

The repetition in "Ruth" thus helps us gauge her spiritual condition of the moment by establishing for us the parameters of her fluctuating soul. Her escape is narrow, and her cure painful, but her ultimate achievement of moral consciousness wins her the Christian burial that we must suppose is meant to suggest that her soul will live on:

> when thy days are told
> Ill-fated Ruth! in hallow'd mold
> Thy corpse shall buried be,
> For thee a funeral bell shall ring,
> And all the congregation sing
> A Christian psalm for thee. (ll. 223–228)

The repetition in "Ruth" also brings us closer than does "Tintern Abbey" to the true figure of thought, which Quintilian distinguishes from the trope, or figure of language.[3] It is of course a matter of degree in Wordsworth,

[3] I discuss this distinction as it relates to Wordsworth in broader perspective in my conclusion. Very briefly, however, Quintilian's distinction between figures of speech or language and figures of thought—a distinction echoed in the eighteenth century by, among others, Campbell and Blair (see George Campbell, *The Philosophy of Rhetoric*, ed. Lloyd F. Bitzer [Carbondale: Southern Illinois University Press, 1963], p. 293; and Blair, *Lectures on Rhetoric*, I, 275–276)—is that figures of thought alone have to do with the "matter"; in oratory, they might be designated as figures expressive of appropriate passion or figures requisite to the adumbration of ideas or logical thought development; in poetics, they might be designated as having thematic interest. In any event they are not merely interesting variant modes of communicating their idea: they *are* the idea. Differences in the degree of thought significance are to be noted in Wordsworth's poetry, a fact that attests to the value of Quintilian's distinction despite

not of kind, for as I have attempted to show, the repetition in "Tintern Abbey" is related to its central concern. The repetition in "Ruth," however, relies less upon "accidents" of language along the way and more upon its broad, preconceived structure, than does the repeating of "green" in "Tintern Abbey," with its reliance upon sounds within other words all along the way. Still more clearly a "figure of thought" is the repetition one finds in "The Brothers," for whereas it makes use of straight reiteration in the manner of "Tintern Abbey," it results in a personification of the rocks which the repetition persistently keeps in the foreground. It is in keeping, perhaps, with his hope of associating certain modes of being with certain natural objects, as expressed in the 1800 Preface, that Wordsworth introduces rock imagery softly, but frequently, into the conversation between Leonard and the Vicar, until by their very familiarity the rocks tend to become presences, rather than mere back-

---

Blair's objection to it (*Lectures on Rhetoric*, I, 275–276). In the final analysis even the distribution of the sounds of "green" and the reiteration of "rocks" in "The Brothers" are of thematic significance, but these instances differ from that of the repetition of "father," for example, in "Ruth," in that they first work on us by making us conscious of them at the verbal level and only in time become relevant to the thought of their poems, whereas the fathers of "Ruth" stand in immediate contrast, owing to their contexts. Another way of describing the difference would be to admit that "green" and "rock" are first tropes, but are finally ironic structures. Quintilian notes that irony can be either a figure of speech or a figure of thought (see Marcus Fabius Quintilian, *Institutio Oratoria*, trans. H. E. Butler [4 vols.; London: William Heinemann, 1922], IX.i.1–7; III, 349–351). The repetition of father in "Ruth," on the other hand, is clearly never a trope, for it does not rely on reiteration, but on ironic contrast. For Quintilian's entire discussion of tropes and figures, see *Institutio Oratoria*, VIII and IX, throughout, and especially IX.ii.44 ff. and IX.iii.88–102 (III, 399 ff. and 499–507).

ground objects. Their omnipresent "faces" speak, for the Vicar, mutely of storms, christenings, separations, boys who knew them intimately, and the dead they have received in their midst.

Of all Wordsworth's imagery, rocks more nearly than any other seem to suggest

> ... certain inherent and indestructible qualities of the human mind, and likewise of certain powers in the great and permanent objects that act upon it which are equally inherent and indestructible.[4]

The Vicar seems to sense that the importance of the rocks lies somehow in their promise of the mind's indestructibility, for he insists, "The thought of death sits easy on the man / Who has been born and dies among the mountains" (lines 183–184). In this consciousness he suits Wordsworth's apparent hope of giving the rocks a voice in "The Brothers," for all his references to the rocks contribute little to what he says, yet they give the Vicar's speech something of the quality of a chronicle recited, as it were, by the rocks themselves. Some of this quality carries over into Leonard's speech as well, for Leonard is of course obliged to humor the Vicar in order to gain the information he wants.

The following selection of lines will give some idea of how naturally the rocks are woven into the conversation, and may help account for the dim sense of life in the rocks which the careful reader, I believe, must feel in reading the poem:

[4] 1800 Preface, in R. L. Brett and A. R. Jones (eds.), *The Lyrical Ballads, 1798 and 1800* (New York: Barnes & Noble, 1963), pp. 243–244.

"Aye, there indeed, your memory is a friend
That does not play you false.—On that tall pike,
(It is the loneliest place of all these hills)
There were two springs."   (ll. 138–141)

                              ". . . or a Shepherd dies
By some untoward death among the rocks."
                                           (ll. 155–156)

                              "who is he that lies
Beneath yon ridge, the last of those three graves;—
It touches on that piece of native rock?"   (ll. 199–201)

                              "—and once I said,
As I remember, looking round these rocks
And hills on which we all of us were born,
That God who made the great book of the world
Would bless such piety—."   (ll. 267–271)

"Leonard and James! I warrant, every corner
Among these rocks and every hollow place
Where foot could come, to one or both of them
Was known."   (ll. 278–281)

                              "ere noon
They found him at the foot of that same Rock
Dead . . . ."   (ll. 392–394)

The "piety" of the two boys is in their love of nature, and
more specifically in that every place among the rocks was
"known" to the boys. Such strong acknowledgment tends
to confer the status of beings upon the rocks; but, more,
their mere appearance at every turn and association with
every event in the poem accomplish much the same end as
the quiet personification of the phrase "to one or both of
them / Was known." Ultimately the rocks, like the color

40

green in "Tintern Abbey," become symbolic; inter-
mediately, however, they become living presences, witnesses
of all that transpires. Knowing this, one shares the full
humor of the Vicar's opening satire at the tourists' expense:

> "some, as wise,
> Upon the forehead of a jutting crag
> Sit perch'd with book and pencil on their knee."
>
> (ll. 5–7)

No doubt they are recording many a picturesque beauty,
but, unlike Leonard, they will leave, having perched on the
very "forehead" of the spirit of the place, without having
given pious recognition, or any recognition, to that spirit
of whose existence they are not even aware. All this becomes
plain, but the subtle animation of the rocks, .the presiding
spirits of the poem, through repetition may not be plain at
the start.

If we do not register the animation of the rocks, the poem
loses for us an important perspective, for each of the three
characters in the poem has a particular relationship to the
rocks, or, more broadly, to the spirit of nature. These
relationships correspond generally to the three Wordsworthian stages of human existence. James, after Leonard's
departure, becomes "the child of all the vale"; the other-
than-literal meaning of this *double-entendre* becomes clear
if we compare him with Ruth, who upon her father's taking
a new mate becomes "an infant of the woods," and with
Lucy, whom nature takes to itself. The conjecture that
James perished among the rocks *while sleepwalking* (as
Ruth sank "through dream and vision") makes the meaning
of his death clear: his spirit was sealed in the sleep of nature,

and nature took him to itself. Leonard separates himself from nature and undergoes the Wordsworthian crisis of imagination; and the Vicar attains a union with nature beyond the crisis stage.

The choice of method in "The Brothers" may be partly responsible for the poem's weaknesses along dramatic lines, for it is sufficiently difficult simply to create convincing speaking roles, without attempting as well to use them to bring symbolic objects to life in the poem. Yet "The Brothers" is an interesting experiment in that the easier way to solve the problem might have been to give the rocks voices outright and not attempt verisimilitude. Byron's solution in *Manfred*, however, would have been unthinkable to Wordsworth, for, aside from the fact that his bent is too literalistic for allegory, straight allegory would have distorted his theme beyond recognition. The drama of man and nature in Wordsworth was to involve ordinary men under nature's habitual influence; Leonard and the Vicar are inhabitants of their region, and not obviously masks worn by the poet. Here, too, it was a question of discovering values in the external world and not simply conferring them upon it: the drama of "The Brothers" is *in* the world, and not simply in Wordsworth's soul.

3

The Intransitive Verb in Wordsworth

Wordsworth's reaction against late eighteenth-century personification, both of abstractions and concrete particulars, is not, as M. H. Abrams points out, to be taken as a turning away from personification itself, but as a reaction against the misuse of it; nor was it, as Abrams also notes, a reaction against the animistic view of nature that had often provided the justification for it. In two separate comments, Abrams conveniently summarizes Wordsworth's reaction:

> Wordsworth's indignation stems from the fact that he himself viewed with a religious reverence those experiences in which he gave a moral life and feeling "to every natural form, rock, fruit, or flower"; these were the high results of his "creative sensibility," and the sovereign resource of his own poetry in its crowning passages. The unforgivable sin of the eighteenth-century poet, therefore, was to use such personification as a rhetorical convention. To Wordsworth's point of view, this dared to alter a natural object in cold blood, without justification in the power of natural and spontaneous passion to enter into, and so remake, the fact it perceives.[1]

[1] Abrams, *The Mirror and the Lamp*, p. 292.

43

What is distinctive in the poetry of Wordsworth and
Coleridge is not the attribution of a life and soul to nature,
but the repeated formulation of this outer life as a con-
tribution of, or else as in constant reciprocation with, the
life and soul of man the observer.[2]

Examples of "cold-blooded" personification are plentiful,
even in those works of the mid-eighteenth century that
Wordsworth held in esteem. Akenside, for example, in a
passage that exhibits the same broad sequence of description
and personification that one finds in many of Wordsworth's
own poems, stands guilty of partially ungenial calculation:

> Behold the expanse
> Of yon gay landscape, where the silver clouds
> Flit o'er the heavens before the sprightly breeze:
> Now their gray cincture skirts the doubtful sun;
> Now streams of splendour, through their opening veil
> Effulgent, sweep from off the gilded lawn
> The aërial shadows; on the curling brook,
> With quickest lustre glancing; while you view
> The prospect, say, within your cheerful breast
> Plays not the lively sense of winning mirth
> With clouds and sunshine chequered, while the round
> Of some gay nymph amid her subject train
> Move all obsequious?[3]

As in many passages in Wordsworth, this begins with an
observed scene, listing and gradually animating its features,
and ends with an "imagination" based on the animated
scene. The un-Wordsworthian quality of the passage is not

[2] *Ibid.*, p. 64.
[3] *Pleasures of Imagination*, III, 292–305, in Robert Anderson (ed.),
The Works of the British Poets (14 vols.; London, 1795), IX, 748.

only its diction (Wordsworth, in *Guilt and Sorrow*, had already begun to put aside this approach to personification before he had quite put aside Akenside's diction), but also the effect wherein the final speculation or "imagination" is felt to determine the personification from the start. That is, in Akenside there is no discovery of nature and no real dialogue with it. The place where "silver clouds / Flit" and "skirt" the sun is too quickly and categorically personified to retain its unique and actual character. Akenside allows the imagined nymph and her train (the spirit of mirth) to supervene from the start, so that the turning of clouds to dresses and all the data subordinated to his topic—a "gay" landscape—is too clearly calculated, too "cold-blooded" for Wordsworth.

To Wordsworth, the mind's self-reflection seen in the animate forms of nature constitutes half of the experience of confronting nature, but the other half is the discovery of a mode of being that is *in nature*; to experience the latter requires a willingness and capacity to recognize the essential otherness of the object which is to reveal that mode of being; it requires both a good eye for detail and a devoted patience in the observing of objects as they actually appear. Not always did Wordsworth include the observed data in his poem, yet implicitly only after a process of close observation and meditation can a fruitful exchange with nature occur. As if in answer to Akenside, Wordsworth writes—

> It is no Spirit who from heaven hath flown
> And is descending on his embassy;
> Nor Traveller gone from earth the heavens to espy!
> 'Tis Hesperus—there he stands . . . .
>
> ("It is no Spirit," ll. 1–4)

To begin to speculate (that is, to personify) too early in the process is necessarily to see nature inexactly and thus to commune not with nature but only with oneself. The clause "there he stands" emphasizes both the otherness of the planet and its animate essence, through the combining of a demonstrative and a personifying pronoun. It introduces a characteristically Wordsworthian pause, which in this case seems to invite us simply to look at the planet, as Wordsworth is doing, in order to observe what it is in its own right; the passage as a whole argues implicitly that if we do so, we too will reject the hasty personifications of the first three lines, for we will see that in fact the planet, to the eye, neither flies, descending, nor mounts anywhere to spy, but simply "stands," which is to say remains in a fixed position. In conjunction with the personifying pronoun "he," the intransitive verb "stands" has also, of course, a personifying effect; but, whereas "he" involves an attribution of life by the observer, "stands" is equivocal, being both an attribution of life and a description of the object as it appears to the eye of the beholder, so that the clause contains both a discovery of life and an attribution of life.

The intransitive verb typically performs two functions in such circumstances: it both suggests the otherness of the object and attributes "life" to it; and insofar as it does both, it tends to suggest that the "life" of the object is *not* an attributed life, but a discovered life. The reader is of course free to deny that a mode of life has been discovered, but if he chooses to do so he shuts himself out of the Wordsworthian transaction between man and nature, either by preferring the conventional notion that poetry's wildest imaginings are true, and that there is no need for exact observation, or by rejecting all notions of a "life of things."

Where the object in Wordsworth is a man, the intransitive verb proves to be a two-edged sword, for it can also approximate man somewhat to the condition of objects in nature. The Wordsworthian vision is a seeing of the middle ground where man and nature approach a common degree of animation; the life of things becomes more evident when the discontinuity between man and nature is overcome, and this can be partially accomplished either by animating things or by de-animating man, so to speak. Sara Hutchinson's insensitivity to the need to decrease the animation of certain poetic figures seems to be Wordsworth's point in taking her to task for not appreciating the fact that in "Resolution and Independence" the old man simply "was."[4] What must have seemed marvelous to William and Dorothy was their encounter, in the flesh, with a man who already simply *was*, that is to say, who had already achieved a certain approximation to the condition of natural objects and who should thus not require a cold-blooded poetic reduction from the ordinary human state of animation to one nearer the state of objects.

As "Resolution and Independence" attests, it is often true of Wordsworth's first-person poems that his characters, though they are opposed to nature and require some "approximating" to it, form part of the fabric of perception from Wordsworth's point of view, or are in other words themselves objects that, along with trees and hills, make up the external world, in relation to which Wordsworth stands as a subject. In the middle portions of their poems, Michael and Ruth, who begin and end as objects in this sense,

---

[4] E. de Selincourt (ed.), *The Early Letters of William and Dorothy Wordsworth* (Oxford: Clarendon Press, 1935), pp. 221–222; see also Jones, *The Egotistical Sublime*, p. 61 ff.

become subjects, so that for a time we view the external world through their eyes. Technically, of course, we are still seeing things through Wordsworth's eyes, but in terms of the imagery they in fact become subjects. The leech-gatherer, however, never becomes a subject in this sense. In terms of the grammar of confrontation between subject and object, what holds true for any natural object holds true as well for the leech-gatherer, with the difference noted earlier that a reverse of personification, a "de-animation," is required to approximate him to the middle condition of Wordsworth's vision, but he actually requires a less strenuous "de-animation" than does Michael.

The "mutual approximation" that Wordsworth discusses in the 1815 Preface, and which involves just this process of personification on the one hand and de-animation on the other, is in a sense a local application of the figure discussed in this chapter. The present chapter broadens the scope of Wordsworth's discussion to include the affiliated processes of straightforward observation and the "fixing" of the object, which in many cases precede the "imagination"; the "imagination" proper is Wordsworth's main concern in the 1815 Preface. Some poems, of course, present only the "imagination," the final portion of the total figure, but a surprising number of poems provide us with the entire confrontation between subject and object. The total figure involves not only the mutual approximation of two things in the external world, but also the mutual approximation of narrator and object—of Wordsworth himself, or a persona such as Michael, and "the Being, that is in the clouds and air."[5]

5 "Hart-leap Well," part ii, l. 165.

A passage that Wordsworth left in manuscript supplies us with the missing preliminary stages of observation and fixation in his encounter with the leech-gatherer:

> My course I stopped as soon as I espied
> The Old Man in that naked wilderness:
> Close by a pond, upon the further side,
> He stood alone: a minute's space I guess
> I watch'd him, he continuing motionless:
> To the Pool's further margin then I drew;
> He being all the while before me full in view.[6]

(ll. 56/57)

A minute is a long, not to mention impolite, interval of staring, but the point is made that exact observation, and presumably a dim recognition of significance in the old man's aspect, are taking place during the interval. What follows in the poem is of course the famous stanza of the mutual approximation of the old man and the stone through the intermediate stage of the sea-beast; stanza ix is the "imagination," and corresponds to Akenside's vision of the nymph and her train. In the above stanza the two stages, those of observation and fixation, are marked by the clauses "my course I stopped" and "he stood alone," which is very like the clause "there he stands" in "It is no Spirit." The difference between the encounter in "It is no Spirit" and that of "Resolution and Independence," however, is that the former ends in the discovery of the animate essence of the planet, whereas the latter ends in the discovery of the affinity between the mind of man and the essence of the enduring objects and the unchanging relationships among

[6] *Poetical Works*, II, 237; stanza reprinted from ms.

things seen and heard at the leech-gatherer's barren spot on the moor. Because of the accident of place, the method of verbally approximating the old man to the condition of the rock becomes for all practical purposes the subject of the poem, for the old man is Man, and the rock and pool are the enduring essences of nature; to "approximate" them is to capture the vision of the mind's permanence perceived in those objects. The grammatical intransitivity opens up into, and is indistinguishable from, the old man's physical intransitivity, that is, "he stood alone" (the grammatical intransitive of the stage of observation) opens up into the physical and imaginative intransitivity of such lines as "motionless as a cloud the old Man stood" (line 75).

Characteristically, however, the encounter is with an object, and the intransitive verb functions only in such a way as to single out the object and to imply that some inherent feature or aspect of it is beginning to fix Wordsworth's attention, as in the clause "there he stands." Occasionally one finds a phrase substituted for the intransitive verb, a phrase that makes the function of the verb even more clear. For example, the phrase "by connecting force / Of their own beauty, imaged in the heart" in the following passage replaces the usual intransitive verb and conveys even more explicitly both the otherness of the object and its peculiar power to fix the attention of the observer:

> such delight I found
> To note in shrub and tree, in stone and flower,
> That intermixture of delicious hues,
> Along so vast a surface, all at once,
> In one impression, by connecting force
> Of their own beauty, imaged in the heart.

—When I had gaz'd perhaps two minutes' space,
Joanna, looking in my eyes, beheld
That ravishment of mine, and laugh'd aloud.

("To Joanna," ll. 45–53)

Corresponding in this case to the "imagination," that is, to Akenside's vision of a nymph or Wordsworth's ordinarily less animated descriptions, is the passage that begins with

The rock, like something starting from a sleep,
Took up the Lady's voice, and laugh'd again.

(ll. 54–55)

This passage of heavy personification, which Coleridge points out was modeled on a passage from Drayton's *Polyolbion*,[7] Wordsworth himself calls an extravagation, a strain of fancy,[8] indicating thereby that having the mountains call to one another is an inappropriately strong way of indicating the "life" he had perceived in the rock; as he puts it, "I was caught in the trap of my own imagination."[9] To put it another way, he fell into personifying in the manner of Akenside, of keeping his attention focused not on the object but on his feeling, his sense of transport.

A highly characteristic example of the present figure is to be noticed in "There is an Eminence." The poem's low key makes it easy to miss its important verbal shifts, but they are there, beginning with the expletive that brings us to a halt before the object ("there is an Eminence,—"), proceeding to the demonstrative mood of fixation ("this Cliff, so high / Above us, and so distant in its height, / Is visible"),

---

[7] Song xxx; see *Biographia Literaria*, II, 82.
[8] *Poetical Works*, II, 487.
[9] *Ibid.*

and culminating in the imaginative animation of the cliff ("and often seems to send / Its own deep quiet to restore our hearts"):

> There is an Eminence,—of these our hills
> The last that parleys with the setting sun.
> We can behold it from our Orchard-seat,
> And, when at evening we pursue our walk
> Along the public way, this Cliff, so high
> Above us, and so distant in its height,
> Is visible, and often seems to send
> Its own deep quiet to restore our hearts.   (ll. 1–8)

We do not attribute personification to the verb "parleys," since it is nearly colloquial, but it softens the way for the gentle personification of the last two lines above. In retrospect we see that "parleys" helps to establish the visual basis of the final image and helps ground the personification in fact, for the quiet which the cliff sends is presumably the reflected sunlight that the cliff takes from the sun in its "parley." Both personifying verbs—"parleys" and "send" —thus have to do with the late evening sunlight.

These lines illustrate something else that happens during the encounter with a natural object, and that is the movement of the outward object into the mind, where it becomes an image, an object in the mind. This movement is marked by what might be called a speculative indicator, usually "seems." As in ordinary conversation, but with a faint note of the prophetic, the Wordsworthian "seems" draws the reader's attention away from the outward object, to which it has been scrupulously affixed, and back toward Wordsworth. The object does not actually disappear from view, for we follow it, as it were, into Wordsworth's mind. The inward movement is usually succeeded, when the object is a thing rather than a person, by personification, if there had been none previously, or by an augmentation of the personification, where there had been. That is to say, the absorbing of the image into the mind of the narrator is followed by an imaginative penetration of the object's essence, a seeing into its "life." The imaginative or speculative insight results, for the reader, in a subjective rendering of the image, for the image, at the point of becoming an inward phenomenon, begins to blend with certain feelings or ideas that had pre-existed in Wordsworth's mind, usually before the encounter.

A model of the experience in its entirety might be useful at this point, to draw some of the loose strands together. Approaching or casually observing a natural object, or in some instances a person, Wordsworth pauses over it, finding his attention fixed by its inherent beauty, or by some unusual quality about it. Having been drawn out of himself, he then discovers signs of volition in the object, sees in it signs of a strange and yet familiar mode of being, or at least in some way becomes cognizant of its otherness, and feels compelled to give it formal recognition. In the poem the recognition often takes the form of a demonstrative and an intransitive verb that receives special poetic emphasis through its favorable position in the line, through rhyme, through an unusual phrasing, or perhaps only by being reinforced imagistically in an intriguing description. Light personification may at times be introduced early and may be part of the formal recognition of the "otherness" of the object, and, if it is, it may contribute to the more forceful personification that so often follows. After an interval of transfixion by the object, a "speculative indicator" such as "seems" marks the reversal of the movement in the poem, a reversal that ends in the complete assimilation of the image and the onset of an imaginative modification of it. The idea of youth, old age, or any of several conceptualizations of modes of human existence generally controls the modification of the image; the result is an animated, a fully personified, or a symbolic image, half-created by its original object and half the embodiment of an abstract idea. If the object is a person, then the individual is seen to have some affinity with symbolic objects in nature.

Lines 11–27 of "A narrow girdle of rough stones" illustrate more clearly than the passages discussed so far the blending of image and idea that results in the special sort of personification one finds in Wordsworth (which is not, in the final analysis, personification, if we grant Wordsworth his premise of a "life of things"). The image containing personification here is that of a thistle seed, and the idea blended with the object is that of youth. The entire figure is encompassed in the following lines:

>   as we strolled along,
> It was our occupation to observe
> Such objects as the waves had toss'd ashore,
> Feather, or leaf, or weed, or wither'd bough,
> Each on the other heap'd along the line
> Of the dry wreck. And in our vacant mood,
> Not seldom did we stop to watch some tuft
> Of dandelion seed or thistle's beard,
> Which, seeming lifeless half, and half impell'd
> By some internal feeling, skimm'd along
> Close to the surface of the lake that lay
> Asleep in a dead calm, ran closely on
> Along the dead calm lake, now here, now there,

In all its sportive wanderings all the while
Making report of an invisible breeze
That was its wings, its chariot, and its horse,
Its very playmate, and its moving soul.

The movement is by starts and jumps here, for the phrase "seeming lifeless half, and half impell'd / By some internal feeling" gives us the speculative indicator, followed immediately by what serves for the intransitive verb ("lifeless half"), and immediately thereupon by the beginnings of personification ("half impell'd / By some internal feeling"). Each stage forwards the next, and the affair quickly runs headlong into speculation. The first blendings are "skimm'd" and "ran." That is, Wordsworth, apparently searching for words that will give due recognition to the object, comes upon two words suggestive of the impetuous movements of youth, the idea to which the object will be joined in the "imagination." The deadness of the lake, twice mentioned, reinforces the notion of youth that is emerging by way of contrast.[10] Thus, by means of an imaginative selection of words, he places the object behind a gauze of associated ideas. The gauze does not alter the image; on the contrary, the object almost seems to give rise to the idea, as though by some inherent human principle in the thistle. Ordinarily in Wordsworth certain features of the modified image correspond with unusual precision to

[10] More important from the standpoint of theme, of course, is the fact that the deadness of Wordsworth's lakes and moors under these circumstances reveals to man his own true nature by indicating that external nature is essentially *not* his soul's true home and that external nature, from man's standpoint, has lulled him into a sleep that is only broken in upon from time to time by such perceptions. For further discussion of this matter, see Chapter VII, parts iii and iv, of the present study.

little-noticed details in the observed object, as already noted in his retaining of the sunlight behind his idea that the cliff sends its "quiet" to him, in "There is an Eminence."

Not unexpectedly, the pattern of the encounter turns up in the earlier poetry, often in much the same terms as those outlined here. In some cases, however, while the pattern of the experience is clearly the same, the verbal structure is not. Where this occurs, the result is sometimes a straightforward account of the experience without benefit of a subject, and therefore without an inward or outward movement. For example, in the following stanza from "The Thorn," one can infer the direction of the movements between perceiver and perceived object, but one has no guidelines; it is as though the sea-captain were giving us *his* account of what happened to *Wordsworth* at the pond:

> "Some say, if to the pond you go,
> And fix on it a steady view,
> The shadow of a babe you trace,
> A baby and a baby's face,
> And that it looks at you;
> Whene'er you look on it, 'tis plain
> The baby looks at you again."   (ll. 225–231)

The initial outward movement of observation ("'if to the pond you go'") and the fixing of the object ("'and fix on it a steady view'") are clear enough, but the beauty of the object is not present here (it is elsewhere in the poem); the mood of the moment of fixation is not appropriate to the Wordsworthian sort of exchange that is transpiring, and the speculative indicator is missing, so that instead of moving gradually into an imagination via "seems," we move directly from "some say" to "'tis plain." All this is appropriate enough in a dramatization of a superstitious mind, but the quality of the experience behind these lines makes it the poet's experience,[11] and yet we find limitations imposed on the verbal resources at Wordsworth's disposal which make of the language an instrument too blunt to convey the true quality of the experience. The failure of this passage from "The Thorn" to treat the confrontation as an imaginatively significant event is not evidence of Wordsworth's lack of technique, for he had already achieved effective poetic "encounters" of its sort; it is only evidence of the almost insurmountable obstacles that dramatic writing imposes on the writer whose material is as deeply personal in some respects as Wordsworth's. As Stephen Parrish has shown, "The Thorn" is a success, dramatically, that is, in the way Wordsworth chiefly hoped it would be; even so, some feel, as Wordsworth must have felt, the lack of that "accumulation of imagery" which the sea-captain, being "destitute of fancy,"[12] cannot supply us with, a lack that surely deprives us of some of the essential intrinsic controls

[11] On the problem of "The Thorn," see first Stephen M. Parrish, "'The Thorn': Wordsworth's Dramatic Monologue," in *ELH*, XXIV (1957), 153–163, and also his "Dramatic Technique in the *Lyrical Ballads*," in *PMLA*, LXXIV (1959), 85–98; see also Albert S. Gérard, "Of Trees and Men: The Unity of Wordsworth's 'The Thorn,'" in *Essays in Criticism*, XIV (1964), 237–255. Gérard sees nature as pointing the sea-captain's way to "the right attitude toward Martha Ray" (p. 249); that is what I take to be at least part of the experience behind the lines I cite from the poem, but it seems to me that the insight must be partly imported by the reader familiar with Wordsworth's theory of nature, that there is no sure way of discovering the theme intrinsically, though I can assent to Gérard's view of the poem. What concerns me is the opacity of individual stanzas, not the force of the poem as a whole, for in this instance there are extrinsic ways of confirming the poem's "meaning."

[12] 1800 note on "The Thorn," in *Poetical Works*, II, 512.

discussed in the present chapter. Even Wordsworth decided that the poem needed a prefatory poem.[13]

Were the tale of Martha Ray an "imagination" in the Akenside sense (which I am convinced it is), and the object seen by the sea-captain no person at all, but a crag and a thorn, the fact would only illustrate further that the sea-captain serves chiefly to block our view of what is really happening in "The Thorn." As susceptible and likable as the sea-captain is, he appears to have aggrandized the poet's attentions and partially divided him in his purpose in the poem, which was to make the thorn a memorable object. The sea-captain finally manages to upstage the thorn, to make himself a more interesting object yet.[14]

[13] *Ibid.*
[14] I. F. note on "The Thorn," in *ibid.*, II, 511–512.

4

Transitive Verbs and Subjective Action

Wordsworth's poetry, generally speaking, is marked by a relatively low proportion of verbs.[1] The fact, however, is anything but indicative of the unimportance of the verb in Wordsworth; the verbs of "Nutting," for example, because they are few, take on a greater importance than they might ordinarily have, and thus perhaps reverse our expectations. The previous chapter endeavors to illustrate how in Wordsworth an added burden is characteristically placed on certain intransitive verbs; this chapter will attempt to show that certain transitive verbs in Wordsworth also occasionally carry more than their usual weight of meaning. The mere fact of a low ratio proves nothing in itself, of course; but it is symptomatic, and, in conjunction with certain other features of the poem it applies to, it contributes to an important and, it would seem, consciously wrought effect in Wordsworth.

Just as "Tintern Abbey" is characteristic of Wordsworth

[1] See Josephine Miles, *Eras and Modes in English Poetry* (Berkeley: University of California Press, 1957), Appendix A; the ratio in "Tintern Abbey" is one verb to every 2.75 nouns, in marked contrast, for example, to Donne's over-all ratio of one verb to one noun. In this regard, Wordsworth and Donne represent extremes.

in its themes, so its verbs of perception and its use of the first person pronoun are characteristic of his manner, which often involves such qualifying clauses as "once again / Do I behold," and "it was our occupation to observe." The first person pronoun occurs in fact with such regularity in Wordsworth that it is one of the prominent stylistic features, and the verbs of perception—especially "see," "hear," "gaze," and "behold"—occur with a corresponding regularity. The first person pronoun and the verbs of perception have the effect of placing Wordsworth in the foreground, of course, and had he wished, he could easily have avoided the effect; we may assume he did not wish to. The activity of nature and of all that is external to Wordsworth consequently tends to be pressed into the background by being grammatically relegated to participial, gerundive, or infinitive phrases. We are not told in "Tintern Abbey" that the waters *roll* from their mountain-springs or that the hedge-rows *run* wild, but that Wordsworth *hears* the waters *rolling* and *sees*, not the hedge-rows that *run* wild, but the hedge-rows that *are run* wild. In these cases the transitive actions are Wordsworth's, and all the other actions (with two exceptions) shade off into adjectival forms of the verb. The pattern of subordinating all but a few actions by means of grammar leaves for a general effect the impression that the ordinary, everyday flush of activity has been in some mysterious way suspended, slowed down, or sometimes even frozen. To say, once again, that the hedge-rows are "run wild" or that the smoke is "sent up" is to render them in a slightly more static way than would be the case if one were to use even the *in*-transitive verbs "runs" and "rises," for the participial forms suggest accomplished facts, not continuing activity.

The pervasive continuing *and* transitive activity is Wordsworth's seeing of all the rest. One or two passages involving the pattern noted here would not have the effect on the reader I have described, but its use in Wordsworth is so consistent that he often appears to depart from it only with the intent of breaking off or playing against the effect for more complex effects.

In the opening lines of "Tintern Abbey," Wordsworth himself is not the only grammatical subject favored with verbs rather than gerunds or participles, for the cliffs and the orchard-tufts also engage in foreground activity, as the verbs in italics below will indicate:

> —once again
> Do I behold these steep and lofty cliffs,
> That on a wild secluded scene *impress*
> Thoughts of more deep seclusion; and *connect*
> The landscape with the quiet of the sky.
> The day is come when I again repose
> Here, under this dark sycamore, and view
> These plots of cottage-ground, these orchard-tufts,
> Which, at this season, with their unripe fruits,
> Among the woods and copses *lose* themselves,
> *Nor*, with their green and simple hue, *disturb*
> The wild green landscape. (ll. 4–15)

While some fact in nature gives rise to the idea that the cliffs "connect" land and sky, the connecting occurs only in Wordsworth's mind and is an aesthetic judgment; in other words, it is a connecting that pertains to the inward and not the outward landscape and is thus a "subjective action." What holds true for "connect" holds true as well for "impress," "lose themselves," and "nor . . . disturb"; their point of reference is in each case the image in Wordsworth's mind, for where else could cliffs impress thoughts? The inward or subjective quality of all these actions becomes even more evident when one realizes that they are all in keeping with Wordsworth's union-in-thought (rather than union-in-sensation) with nature; he has come to an awareness of a "presence" or a "sense" (assuming the two terms to be in apposition)[2] whose "dwelling" (strange to say) is not only in nature, but in the mind as well. Generally speaking, the topic of the opening landscape is that of a harmony discovered in nature which corresponds to the inward tranquillity he feels. The "subjective" verbs noted here single out the internal qua external agents of that tranquillity. "Green," as noted earlier (see Chapter II), is the tranquillity of the landscape in the mind; the cliffs and tufts are the spirits of the place, the agents manipulating the interfusions and bringing about harmony and tranquillity. In making their actions transitive, moreover, Wordsworth aligns their actions with his own acts of perceiving and thus divorces them from other objects whose actions are not set down in transitive verbs.

The cliffs and tufts are thus expressive features of the landscape of the mind. The other data are relevant, but it is the cliffs, not the hedge-rows or sky, that function actively to harmonize the inward landscape. The cliffs and tufts do not stand out so much visually as they do grammatically,

[2] See William Empson, *Seven Types of Ambiguity* (2nd ed.; London: Chatto & Windus, 1949), pp. 151–154; Empson is correct about the ambiguity, but does not seek the perspective that other parts of the poem provide and which makes the ambiguity rich, not puzzling. Empson seems almost sorry that there is ambiguity in that he (Empson) is thus prevented from assailing Wordsworth's pantheism.

and in this way they resemble the *spirit* of nature which, like the breeze, is not seen, but rather felt.

The poetic effect wrought by Wordsworth's unusual distribution of verbs is that of a kind of understatement which sensitizes the reader to the slightest of shifts toward or away from foreground activity and transitiveness as expressed by his verbs. One of the more delicately managed poems illustrating this quality is "Nutting," a poem that is fortunately short enough so that something of the full intricacy of its verb structure can be shown without too lengthy an explication. The poem turns upon an encounter between the young Wordsworth and the spirit of nature, or, more particularly, the *genius loci* of the hazel bower. With its "temptation" and its "merciless ravage," the encounter takes on the color of a combat, but it is, of course, in reality a psychic exchange which is simply at one point dramatized by a physical action; yet the principle of hostility is significant.

The poem's over-all quality of suspended action is attributable to its extraordinarily low ratio of verbs to nouns.[3] This quality is most marked in the opening section:

> It seems a day
> (I speak of one from many singled out)
> One of those heavenly days which cannot die,
> When forth I sallied from our cottage-door,
> And with a wallet o'er my shoulder slung,
> A nutting crook in hand, I turn'd my steps
> Towards the distant woods, a Figure quaint,
> Trick'd out in proud disguise of Beggar's weeds
> Put on for the occasion, by advice
> And exhortation of my frugal Dame.

[3] To be precise, the ratio is one verb to 3.5 nouns; see footnote 1 above.

Motley accoutrement! of power to smile
At thorns, and brakes, and brambles, and, in truth,
More ragged than need was. Among the woods,
And o'er the pathless rocks, I forc'd my way
Until, at length, I came to one dear nook
Unvisited, where not a broken bough
Droop'd with its wither'd leaves, ungracious sign
Of devastation, but the hazels rose
Tall and erect, with milk-white clusters hung,
A Virgin scene!   (ll. 1–20)

Beginning with "When forth I sallied," the verbs are "sallied," "turn'd," "was," "forc'd," "came," "droop'd," and "rose." Wordsworth later changes "sallied" to "left" and drops the verb "forc'd," and since "need was" is little more than a poetic improvement upon "necessary," the verb "was" can perhaps be overlooked in an examination of the verbs in the passage (those verbs, that is, which predicate the main actions, and exclusive of adjectival, gerundive, and participial forms). The list that remains is "left," "turn'd," "came," "droop'd," and "rose," a very short and very colorless list of verbs to build sixteen lines of verse on! All are in effect intransitive (the phrase "turn'd my steps" involves a technically transitive verb, but the action as a whole is intransitive). As in "I came, I saw, I conquered," all are in a sense gestures, being more important with respect to establishing the posture of their subjects than to establishing a significant relationship between grammatical subjects and objects. Moreover, all are divided between just two subjects—Wordsworth and the hazels. The effect thus becomes one of gesture and counter-gesture between the two rival subjects, with the rest of the activity in the passage falling away from the main sequence of actions, which is as follows: "I left," "I turn'd," and "I came"; and then "not a broken bough droop'd" and "the hazels rose." In this way, Wordsworth and the hazels are disengaged from the tapestry of incidental activity and stand ready for their encounter on a new plane of action.

The shift to transitive verbs, beginning with the phrase "eyed the banquet" (lines 23–24), marks the onset of action on the new plane, the beginning of the "subjective action" of the poem. Having been singled out by the intransitive verbs, Wordsworth and the hazels (which rise to the occasion, as it were, like guardian spirits of the place) from here on to the end of the episode divide the transitive actions between themselves. The bower appears to have two aspects, the hazels, or outward bower, and the nook, or inward bower, but just one "being," and in this outward-inward aspect it parallels the young poet who is to discover its being.

The breaking of the bough is of course the climax of the exchange. While it may appear to be the first sign of interchange, it is actually anticipated in the transitive verbs that precede the climactic verb "dragg'd." The "subjective action" can be outlined by noting the transitive verbs and their objects, which are italicized in the passage that follows:

—A little while I stood,
Breathing with such suppression of the heart
As joy delights in; and with wise restraint
Voluptuous, fearless of a rival, *eyed*
The banquet, or beneath the trees I sate
Among the flowers, and with the flowers I play'd;
A temper known to those, who, after long
And weary expectation, have been bless'd
With sudden happiness beyond all hope.—

Perhaps it was a bower beneath whose leaves
The violets of five seasons re-appear
And fade, unseen by any human eye,
Where fairy water-breaks do murmur on
For ever, and *I saw the sparkling foam*,
And with my cheek on one of those green stones
That, fleec'd with moss, beneath the shady trees,
Lay round me scatter'd like a flock of sheep,
I heard the murmur and the murmuring sound,
In that sweet mood when pleasure loves to pay
Tribute to ease, and, of its joy secure,
The heart luxuriates with indifferent things,
Wasting its kindliness on stocks and stones,
And on the vacant air. Then up I rose,
And *dragg'd to earth both branch and bough*, with crash
And merciless ravage; and the shady nook
Of hazels, and the green and mossy bower
Deform'd and sullied, patiently *gave up*
Their quiet being.   (ll. 20–47)

The bower's giving up of its being is of course a reflexive
action, unless we distinguish between its "body" and "soul"
(which we probably should do, in accordance with Wordsworth's division of it, noted earlier, into outward and
inward aspects), but since a bower is supposedly inanimate,
that it should *do* anything is significant in that it strikes us as
more "transitive" than we should have expected. It is clearly
Wordsworth's sense of the bower's having done something
that fixes in his mind the notion that there is "a Spirit in the
woods" (line 55). Thus, whereas the intransitive verbs serve
to subordinate incidental activity, the transitive verbs
advance the "subjective action" between the two beings
that emerge grammatically from the tapestry of Wordsworth's language.

66

The eyeing, seeing, and hearing in the bower are telling actions; they are what appears to provoke the interaction, though nature has clearly tempted the young Wordsworth.[4] The actions bear overtones of transgression for the reader of mythology, who rather expects the young Wordsworth to be transformed into a stag. Harold Bloom's hypothesis of a sexual transgression, however, perhaps offers us a more appropriate way to view the event; it is not, of course, inconsistent with the mythological view, but it goes further toward describing sensitively the mood of the episode.[5] Yet, as Alan Grob has more recently maintained, Wordsworth's meaning carries us beyond sexual violation. Grob argues that by introducing overtones of sexual violation, Wordsworth is able to translate a nature experience into a moral experience.[6] I would add, in support of this last interpretation, that the poem's sexual overtones provide only the metaphor and that the exchange must be understood as taking place between the only two participants of every "subjective action" in Wordsworth—man and nature.

The most fundamental of oppositions is always between these two, whatever relationship between man and man is introduced into the poem. This duality becomes more clearly than ever the only relevant one in the overflow portions of "Nutting," where Wordsworth comes very close to describing himself at the moment of breaking the bough:

[4] For a defense of the last view expressed, see Alan Grob, "Wordsworth's 'Nutting,'" in *Journal of English and Germanic Philology*, LXI (1962), 826–832.

[5] Harold Bloom, *The Visionary Company: A Reading of English Romantic Poetry* (New York: Doubleday & Co., 1961), pp. 136–139.

[6] Grob, "Wordsworth's 'Nutting,'" p. 828.

If I had met thee here with that keen look
Half cruel in its eagerness, those cheeks
Thus [   ] flushed with a tempestuous bloom,
I might have almost deem'd that I had pass'd
A houseless being in a human shape,
An enemy of nature.[7]

There is a fundamental antagonism in "Nutting" between the alien soul of man, who has not yet forgotten "that imperial palace whence he came," and nature, which does all in its power to establish in man a "primal sympathy" that will make co-existence possible. When necessary, nature meets force with force, and works to subdue the soul. The verbs of "Nutting" reflect the more violent sort of transaction that one finds in Wordsworth. They do not personify nature in the ordinary sense of the word in spite of all the interaction, for none but the last places the least strain on idiomatic usage. Wordsworth's method of animating nature sufficiently to single it out for an exchange with man is his consistent separation of the planes of action predicated through transitive verb, intransitive verb, and verbal substantive or modifier. If "Nutting" is any indication, Wordsworth either composed with a good deal more care than he wishes us to think, or his grammatical sense and memory were truly extraordinary.

[7] *Poetical Works*, II, 505; ll. 8–13.

5

Synecdoche in "Michael"

Directness of expression forms no part of the plainness of
the style of "Michael"; even at the beginning, Wordsworth
uses more circumlocution and periodic ordination than one
may be conscious of in cursory readings:

> If from the public way you turn your steps
> Up the tumultuous brook of Green head Gill,
> You will suppose that with an upright path
> Your feet must struggle; in such bold ascent
> The pastoral Mountains front you, face to face.
> But courage! for beside that boisterous Brook
> The mountains have all open'd out themselves,
> And made a hidden valley of their own.
> No habitation there is seen; but such
> As journey thither find themselves alone
> With a few sheep, with rocks and stones, and kites
> That overhead are sailing in the sky.   (ll. 1–12)

In the first line, "turn" is expanded into "turn your steps,"
and in the fourth line, "you must struggle" becomes "your
feet must struggle." These expanded phrasings and the
suspension of the main clause lend the passage a certain
elegance, a sort of guidebook punctilio. Since Wordsworth

is our guide, the style is of course fitting; yet, one may notice that both of the circumlocutions cited quietly urge our divisibility as persons into "selves" on the one hand and "bodily extremities" on the other. The effect is so slight, and the phrases so seemingly commonplace, that the attentive reader who catches it might dismiss it as insignificant. It is closely followed up, however, by a curiously correspondent divisibility in nature, for the upright path and face of the mountains conceal a "hidden valley," an inward recess and fit habitation, as it were, for the soul of nature. The language of "Michael" is not merely indirect: the selection and arrangement of the language of its opening lines prefigure its drama, its confrontation between man and nature.

A clear pattern of interaction emerges in the lines that follow and in the tale of Michael, for natural objects continue to be slightly personified and the overscrupulous locution of "your feet must struggle" continues to find its way into the expression in what may add up to a uniquely Wordsworthian use of synecdoche. The main drama involves Michael and nature, of course, and synecdoche enters the poem most noticeably in connection with Wordsworth's characterization of Michael.

Our knowledge of Michael is largely our knowledge of his relationship with his surroundings. For example, in the following passages Michael is not delineated; natural objects are simply grouped around him, and we infer what he is from where he is:

> the storm, that drives
> The Traveller to a shelter, summon'd him
> Up to the mountains: he had been alone
> Amid the heart of many thousand mists;   (ll. 56–59)

> he sate
> With sheep before him on his Shepherd's stool,
> Beneath that large old Oak, which near their door
> Stood;   (ll. 173–176)

> Near the tumultuous brook of Green-head Gill,
> In that deep Valley, Michael had design'd
> To build a Sheep-fold.   (ll. 332–334)

Even the inversion of the opening sentence of the tale of Michael seems designed to lend primacy to the setting rather than to the person of Michael:

> Upon the Forest-side in Grasmere Vale
> There dwelt a Shepherd, Michael was his name;
>   (ll. 40–41)

and of course the entire tale of Michael is framed by natural description.

Our sense of being alone with natural objects is maintained throughout the poem by the frequent synecdoches, through which Wordsworth brings into play a kind of movement from the self "outward" toward ear, eye, hand, and natural object. It is significant that Wordsworth seldom stops with his synecdochic counter, but instead moves beyond the hand, for example, to what it touches, for it is this further movement that keeps us, with Michael, ever alone amid natural objects. The three important terms— the terms indicating the self, the adjunct, and the natural object—are italicized in each of the following instances:

> *She* was a woman of a stirring life
> Whose *heart* was in her *house*;   (ll. 83–84)

71

Michael telling o'er his years began
To deem that *he* was old, in Shepherd's phrase,
With one *foot* in the *grave*;   (ll. 90–92)

both betook themselves
To such convenient work, as might employ
Their *hands* by the *fire-side*;   (ll. 106–108)

[There]
Would *Michael* exercise his heart with *looks*
Of fond correction and reproof bestowed
Upon the *child*;   (ll. 182–184)

from *the Boy* there came
Feelings and emanations, things which were
Light to the *sun* and music to the *wind*;   (ll. 210–212)

"And still *I* lov'd thee with encreasing love.
Never to living *ear* came sweeter *sounds*";   (ll. 354–355)

"*they* were not loth
To give their *bodies* to the family *mold.*"   (ll. 379–380)

Some of the above instances will strike the reader, rightly, as not being synecdochic at all—rightly, that is, unless he has discovered that in Wordsworth such things as the "bodies" of the last instance and the "feelings and emanations" of the fifth may feasibly be weighed as adjuncts of the self. However, these instances illustrate one of the primary difficulties in considering the figurative aspects of his language, which is his habit of slipping without notice from a rhetorical bestowal, for example, into a literal bestowal. One imagines that to Wordsworth all of the above instances were bestowals, literal givings, and none a mere figure of speech; and it would seem that we must make some effort to adopt his view before we can appreciate to the full the burden and the beauty of language as Wordsworth conceived of it. In any event, the theme of "Michael" is ultimately indistinct from its language.

The synecdochic movement in "Michael" contributes to our sense of a mutual approximation of man and nature toward a middle condition in that it draws our attention for the moment away from the mutually exclusive realms of man and nature and focuses it on the converging realms of eye and object. The gentle personification of "Michael" introduces an opposed but complementary movement, for it draws our attention away from a nature that is distinct from man and focuses it on a nature viewed as dimly animate and thus approximated to the human. Again, Wordsworth's method of personifying is to move almost imperceptibly from ordinary language into subtle arrangements and heightenings. The expression "face to face" (line 5) is characteristic, in that by itself it would hardly constitute poetic personification; yet, when one notices how frequently the language is punctuated with personifying words and how tightly they interlock, one sees in retrospect the true color of even the least conspicuous or most idiomatic of the poem's personifying words.

One of the slightly disguised concerns of lines 13–39 is to prepare us to understand aright the subsequent personifications by implanting the notion that nature actively engages man and leads him to love his fellow men and that tales such as that of Michael, by linking human passions to natural objects, continue this work of nature. The tale of Michael was one

> that spoke to me
> Of Shepherds, dwellers in the valleys, men
> Whom I already lov'd, not verily
> For their own sakes, but for the fields and hills.
>
> (ll. 22–25)

By separating the story of Michael from all tincture of books or bookishness, Wordsworth loosens our habit of distinguishing between the human and the natural on the conceptual plane, for art and nature, agency and power, become so interwoven in our thoughts that discrimination is rendered difficult:

> And hence this Tale, while I was yet a boy
> Careless of books, yet having felt the power
> Of Nature, by the gentle agency
> Of natural objects led me on to feel
> For passions that were not my own.   (ll. 27–31)

The prose sense of this passage is that the tale of Michael taught Wordsworth sympathy for Michael and that its power to do so resided in the natural objects it depicted, in conjunction with Wordsworth's susceptibilities. One is invited to conclude that the tale, the verbalization, was merely the husk, the disguise that nature used to gain a secondary entrance to his mind.

Lines 13–39 thus hint that the essential tale of Michael is in the stones of the sheepfold and that Wordsworth's function was to depict those stones as exactly as he could. The task was not at all simple, of course, but required an imaginative penetration of the stones, an evincing of their history, their meaning for us, their very life. Accordingly, the result of this process would be the poem as we know it,

and the "life" of the stones—the shepherd, Michael.
Between the lines of "Michael" one again discovers Wordsworth's curiously literal belief in the "life of things." There
is a manner-of-speaking explanation for the lines—

> There is a straggling heap of unhewn stones!
> And to that place a story appertains;   (ll. 17–18)

and for the lines—

>   [hills]
> Which like a book preserv'd the memory
> Of the dumb animals, whom he had sav'd;   (ll. 70–71)

but for the careful reader of "The Thorn" and "Michael"
the following lines from *The Prelude* are more than metaphoric:

>   even then I felt
> Gleams like the flashing of a shield;—the earth
> And common face of Nature spake to me
> Rememberable things.   (1850; I, 585–588)

In reading lines 13–39, we take the path of least resistance
if we posit an unseen being who speaks to man by means of a
symbolic language consisting of memorable natural objects.

Lines 40–80 of "Michael" proceed gradually from a low
to a high pitch of concrete personification. Ostensibly, these
lines characterize Michael's mode of existence, specifically
in relation to nature; in fact, however, they establish nature
as a second participant in the action by subtly personifying
natural objects and giving them a grammatical initiative in
the relationship between Michael and nature, as indicated by
the italicized verbs in the following passage:

75

The Shepherd, at such warning, of his flock
Bethought him, and he to himself would say
The winds *are now devising* work for me!
And truly at all times the storm, that *drives*
The Traveller to a shelter, *summon'd* him
Up to the mountains: he had been alone
Amid the heart of many thousand mists
That *came* to him and *left* him on the heights.
So liv'd he till his eightieth year was pass'd.
  And grossly that man errs, who should suppose
That the green Valleys, and the Streams and Rocks
Were things indifferent to the Shepherd's thoughts.
Fields, where with chearful spirits he had breath'd
The common air; the hills which he so oft
Had climb'd with vigorous steps; which *had impress'd*
So many incidents upon his mind
Of hardship, skill or courage, joy or fear;
Which like a book *preserv'd* the memory
Of the dumb animals, whom he had sav'd,
Had fed or shelter'd, linking to such acts,
So grateful in themselves, the certainty
Of honorable gains; these fields, these hills
Which were his living Being, even more
Than his own Blood—what could they less?—*had laid*
Strong hold on his affections, were to him
A pleasurable feeling of blind love,
The pleasure which there is in life itself.   (ll. 53–79)

Animation is achieved in these lines almost without our
being at first aware of it, for none of the italicized verbs
deviates widely in its effect from that of the unavoidable
obsolete personifying words that sprinkle the language.
From the standpoint of personification, the chief difference
between these lines and common speech is that in common
speech one is not likely to personify one kind of entity with

great frequency. Mists are commonly said to "come" to one or "leave" one, and the shapes of hills might be thought to evoke memories and so be said to have "impressed" certain incidents on the mind; but to insist in the same breath that they also "linked," "preserved," and "laid hold on" would be to introduce more weight of personification than common speech can bear without showing signs of strain: we would recognize, on the basis of personification alone, that poetry is urging its way into speech, as we do in the passage above from "Michael." Wordsworth has managed, however, to blend the two—poetry and speech—very adroitly. The secret of lines 40–80 may lie in the supporting oratorical crescendo, in their gradual progression from hesitant to balanced phrasings.

The special virtue of the personification of these lines might be instanced most clearly by contrast. In "The Brothers," Wordsworth attempts in somewhat the same way to give a life to objects, but fails: the Vicar, one will recall, refers to one of the "brother fountains" as "dead and gone" (see lines 141–146); the reason the line fails is not that in this instance personification, the "pathetic fallacy," is fallacious, but that in this instance "dead and gone" does not blend into its speech-context. Where personification in Wordsworth is not supported by a close network of animating words and justified by the speaker's passion, it becomes not pathetic but bathetic, for Wordsworth was the poet of man speaking to man. The Vicar might have said "dried up," "disappeared," or even "died away," but not the weeping phrase "dead and gone." Blair, Shenstone, Blake, even Yeats or Thomas, might have been able to supply the context for Wordsworth's "dead and gone," for they depend less than does Wordsworth upon the common idiom to wed fact and vision.

The digression on the lamp in "Michael" (lines 112–124), like the introduction to Michael of lines 40–80, also provides an element of characterization, but exists more particularly for its personification, this time of "natural" objects within doors. As in those instances of man-made edifices fallen into decay, familiar household objects worn to a state of comfortable ruin may in Wordsworth be deemed "natural." I have again italicized the significant personifying words:

> Down from the ceiling by the chimney's edge,
> Which in our ancient uncouth country style
> Did with a huge projection *overbrow*
> Large space beneath, as duly as the light
> Of day grew dim, the House-wife hung a lamp;
> An *aged* utensil, which had perform'd
> Service beyond all others of its kind.
> Early at evening did it burn and late,
> *Surviving Comrade* of uncounted *Hours*
> Which *going by* from year to year *had found*
> And *left* the Couple neither gay perhaps
> Nor chearful, yet *with* objects and *with* hopes
> *Living* a life of eager industry.

The fireplace, the lamp, the very hours and hopes of the old couple comprise a kind of society that crosses the boundaries of the human and the natural. Such personification of unexpected entities, such subtle humanizing of things, is characteristic of Wordsworth at his best. In this particular case his method serves admirably to introduce nature as a presence even into areas of their existence in which Michael and Isabel are out of reach of the influence of trees and sky. The lamp, seen from the valley, so resembles the evening star that the dwellers in the valley name the cottage for the star, in acknowledgment of the resemblance. The lamp is an inward phenomenon, like the "hidden valley" where the sheepfold is, a kind of indoor light of nature, which, like the mind, has its outward or heavenly counterpart.

Synecdoche and personification in "Michael" thus serve to bring Michael and nature into a close relationship; one might conceive of the two aspects of method as introducing opposed but complementary verbal "movements" that draw Michael and nature toward a common center of being. The "action" of the poem, which is contained in these movements, resembles that of "Tintern Abbey," for it involves a change in Michael's relationship with nature. Before Luke's birth, Michael's feeling with regard to nature is that of a "blind" attraction ("a pleasurable feeling of blind love" [line 78]); it is in this respect analogous to Wordsworth's reported feeling with regard to nature in his youth:

> I cannot paint
> What then I was. The sounding cataract
> Haunted me like a passion: the tall rock,
> The mountain, and the deep and gloomy wood,
> Their colours and their forms, were then to me
> An appetite: a feeling and a love.
>
> ("Tintern Abbey," ll. 76–81)

In "Michael," Luke's coming marks the familiar temporary separation of Michael from nature, or what might be called more accurately the sublimation of the love of nature into the love of man:

> to the thoughts
> Of the old Man his only Son was now
> The dearest object that he knew on earth.
>
> (ll. 158–160)

Wordsworth later sharpened his theme of nature leading beyond itself, toward social love, by adding of Luke that he was one of the "gifts / (That earth can offer to declining man)" (1832, lines 150–151). Like Lucy, Luke prismatically refracts the beauty of nature and thus draws Michael's affections away from nature and toward man. Michael is thus reborn through Luke (line 213): the music he now hears is not subterraneous (line 51), issuing from the wind; it is an emanation from Luke that is "music to the wind" (line 212).

Luke's subsequent defection throws Michael back upon nature, but his new relationship with nature is different from the old: Michael cannot return to a "blind" love of nature; he can only move on to a stoic and spiritual partnership with it, a love based not on sensation, but on thought. The changed quality of his relationship with nature at the end of the poem is suggested by a changed quality in the imagery: in the beginning, nature had been mists, streams, and fields; in the end, it is naked rocks and sun. Yet, in the end, love of nature and love of man exist for Michael in their truest form.

Toward the end of the poem, synecdoche and personification drop away, for the approximation has been accomplished. In the memorable final portion of the tale of Michael, Michael and nature are in essential communion; they are no longer separated by natural object and bodily eye, for Michael has discovered in himself a power of love that requires no prop in sensation, and nature stands revealed to him as a presence which had been only temporarily concealed by the shifting elements. The two commune directly by the heart-shaped "straggling heap of stones" with which the poem begins and ends.

6

Characters of Place:
Similes and Personification

Readers of Wordsworth must certainly have experienced sometime the disappointment of plucking some flower from Wordsworth's poetry, only to have it wilt amid new surroundings. One thinks of the lines

> Poor Matthew, all his frolics o'er,
> Is silent as a standing pool.
>
> ("If Nature, for a favorite child")

While these particular lines may not strike one as attractive even in context, they illustrate the wilting tendency in that whereas they fit comfortably into their poem, outside of it they put up a poor show. By no means all of Wordsworth's similes are so unimpressive as this out of context; yet, as often as not, Wordsworth's are less impressive than even their fair to middling Elizabethan counterparts. Sidney, for example, in the following lines, turns to advantage a fairly commonplace comparison of face and sky:

> Stella oft sees the very face of woe
> Painted in my beclouded stormy face,
> But cannot skill to pity my disgrace.
>
> (*Astrophel and Stella*, xlv)

Using the same basic comparison, Wordsworth writes—

> There sits he: in his face you spy
> No trace of a ferocious air,
> Nor ever was a cloudless sky
> So steady or so fair.
>
> ("The Danish Boy," ll. 56–59)

Rhythmically, the last two lines above by Wordsworth are strong and round out the simile very nicely; there is, however, a quality of overbalance to the simile that works in nature's favor, owing to the fact that the image of face and that of sky succeed one another, that of the sky coming last, and to the fact that the image of the face is presented negatively ("no trace of a ferocious air"), whereas the sky is given particular qualities. Since the two images are not interwoven, the transference from sky to face is not total, as it is in Sidney's lines.

As usual in Wordsworth, one must move outward from particular facts to relationships in order to account for the power he can exert on us in spite of what might appear to be momentary lapses of expression. A look at the rest of "The Danish Boy" will indicate that the effect of an over-balance in favor of nature characterizes all of its similes and tends to make the particular lines cited less uncomfortable in context. The virtue of all the similes becomes clear only when we see the structure they help support, and of which they form an inextricable part. Whereas the beauty of Sidney's lines is that they enable us to view his face through nature and thus see it more clearly, the beauty of Wordsworth's is that they enable us to view nature through a human being and thus see *nature* more clearly. The other similes in "The Danish Boy" are if anything less particular concerning the boy and more particular about the setting than are those cited. Since we are not accustomed to seeing boys dressed in fur, we may be deceived in this, but to one so accustomed, surely the quality of overbalance in the similes would be clear in the following lines:

> A regal vest of fur he wears,
> In color like the raven's wing;
> It fears nor rain, nor wind, nor dew,
> But in the storm 'tis fresh and blue
> As budding pines in Spring. (ll. 27–31)

We do not know what form "The Danish Boy" might have taken, had Wordsworth finished it, but from what we have of it, it is clear that the setting was to play an important part in it.

Frequently Wordsworth's similes, taken collectively in a given poem, integrate or unify a scene, rather than a person, and in this respect they contrast not only with Elizabethan similes but also with those of many a morally integrated and extended character description in the poetry of the eighteenth century. The latter are typified by the following passage from Crabbe:

> Oft may you see him, when he tends the sheep,
> His winter-charge, beneath the hillock weep;
> Oft hear his murmur to the winds that blow
> O'er his white locks and bury them in snow,
> When, roused by rage and muttering in the morn,
> He mends the broken hedge with icy thorn:—
> "Why do I live, when I desire to be
> At once from life, and life's long labor free?

Like leaves in spring, the young are blown away,
Without the sorrows of a slow decay;
I, like yon wither'd leaf, remain behind,
Nipped by the frost, and shivering in the wind."
(The Village, I, 200–211)

As in Sidney, there is in Crabbe a sustained quality to the
satiric matter and a discontinuous quality to the descriptive
matter that places him in a different tradition from that in
which Wordsworth writes. However faceless or un-
differentiated Crabbe's characters may be, as they seldom
are, of the two heterologous realms—the human and the
natural—which his similes draw upon, the human is
unmistakably the more integrated. The imagery is highly
consistent, and yet it is assembled with the clear intent of
strengthening the poem's moral topic and of making the
old man's time of life and the quality of his suffering more
vivid. By contrast, the similes of "The Danish Boy" leave
us with but a vague notion of the boy's character, his
motivation, and even, finally, his physiognomy; on the
other hand, they do leave us with a definite sense of the
place, of the storm that has recently passed, the pines and
ravens, the season, and even the time of day ("A spirit of
noon day is he" [line 23]).

"The Danish Boy" is by no means the only poem by
Wordsworth in which the setting is made more recog-
nizable through the similes than is the person those similes
supposedly help depict. The question of Lucy's identity
will probably never be resolved by internal evidence, for
while her setting and often the time of day are plain,[1] such

[1] See F. W. Bateson, *Wordsworth: a Reinterpretation* (2nd ed.;
London: Longmans, Green & Co., 1956), pp. 33–35; Bateson notes

84

lines as the following can be of no help in identifying her as
a historical personage:

> A Violet by a mossy stone
> Half-hidden from the Eye!
> —Fair, as a star when only one
> Is shining in the sky!
> ("She dwelt among the untrodden ways")

Matthew's "blooming Girl" in "The Two April Mornings"
is also, like Lucy, rendered nearly invisible by the similes
that ostensibly describe her, and she, too, emerges as a kind
of creature of the mood and place, a being who is both less
than and more than a person:

> And, turning from her grave, I met
> Beside the church-yard Yew
> A blooming Girl, whose hair was wet
> With points of morning dew.
>
> A basket on her head she bare,
> Her brow was smooth and white,
> To see a Child so very fair,
> It was a pure delight!
>
> No fountain from its rocky cave
> E'er tripp'd with foot so free,
> She seem'd as happy as a wave
> That dances on the sea.   (ll. 41–52)

While there is no straining to conceal the girl's appearance,
from the word "blooming" on, the image of a flower seems

the specificity of place and time of day in "She dwelt among the
untrodden ways" and gives the fact an interesting interpretation,
according to which Lucy symbolically aggrandizes the images of the
setting, indeed "*is* the whole evening scene."

to govern the description, and where the detail strives most for particularity it leaves the girl and paints the scene instead, so that all we finally see of her is the dew in her hair and the whiteness of her forehead. The yew in the churchyard overlooking a sea with waves, in view of mountains and a stream—the total scene, drawn at a particular hour of the day, just before the dew has risen—has certainly as much to do with Matthew's feeling of the moment as the girl herself. These lovely stanzas demonstrate that the use of similes to construct integrated settings need not result in awkward or unmemorable similes.

It might be useful to turn aside, for the moment, from the more or less limited and technical approach employed thus far and take up a matter that, while not directly relevant to style, may cast some light on Wordsworth's use of setting, which in turn affects his style. The relationship between Wordsworth's characters and his places is made tighter as a result of the "mutual approximations" that each of the devices looked at so far, but especially the simile, contributes to; that relationship in fact tends to become so tight that it may be more profitable to speak not of character *and* setting in Wordsworth, as though they were quite separate considerations, but instead of his "characters of place."

It would seem to be wrong to assume, because setting is as important as it is in Wordsworth, that "character" is not important. Indeed, it might be closer to the truth to say that in a very deep sense character is for Wordsworth the primary consideration in every poem and that he is simply approaching the moral integration of his matter in a different way than Crabbe. Although they often do not measure up as realistic figures in the dramatic sense, Wordsworth's characters do illustrate both the possibility and value of rediscovering man in nature and through nature. What one appears to be dealing with in Wordsworth are not unique individuals but modes of being, something closer to Samuel Johnson's general nature than to the character particularity we demand in the novel. As was indicated in relation to "Michael," Wordsworth's particularity about his characters, even in his notes, it might be added, is somewhat misleading; more often than not, what he is particular about is a place. The modes of being he is concerned with are usually men seen, not face to face, but by the mind's eye, men exalted through their association with certain impressive or enduring forms of nature.

In a letter to Coleridge dating from the Goslar period, Wordsworth indicates that he was at that time considering in some depth the problem of characterization and its relationship to natural description. Wordsworth writes:

> I do not so ardently desire character in poems like Burger's, as manners, not transitory manners reflecting the wearisome unintelligible obliquities of city life, but manners connected with the permanent objects of nature and partaking of the simplicity of those objects. Such pictures must interest when the original shall cease to exist. The reason will be immediately obvious if you consider yourself as lying in a valley on the side of mount Etna reading one of Theocritus's Idylliums or on the plains of Attica with a comedy of Aristophanes in your hand. Of Theocritus and his spirit perhaps three fourths remain, of Aristophanes a mutilated skeleton; at least I suppose so, for I never read his works but in a most villainous translation. But I may go further, read Theocritus in Ayrshire or Merionethshire and you will find perpetual occasions to recollect what you

daily see in Ayrshire or Merionethshire, read Congreve[,] Vanbrugh and Farquhar in London and though not a century has elapsed since they were alive and merry, you will meet with whole pages that are uninteresting and incomprehensible. Now I find no manners in Burger . . . .[2]

The characters Wordsworth objects to in Bürger are to some extent those of his own earlier ballads, although even in 1798 Wordsworth was clearly in search of a principle of characterization that might render narrative incident obsolete in the ballad (see "Simon Lee," stanza ix). The point of his wish for "manners" appears to be his concern with what I have termed "modes of being," to distinguish them from "characterization" even in the best sense in Restoration practice. In any event the poetry that was to follow does not even attempt to abstract principles of general human nature from a study of society; instead, it applies Samuel Johnson's notion of general nature in a way that would have surprised the Johnson who faced Dryden and Pope, for it turns directly to tree, hill, and valley—not of Etna, but of Grasmere—as to its laboratory for the distilling of character, to rural nature!

There is indication in the following passage from *The Prelude* (a passage probably related genetically to "Michael") that early in his life Wordsworth had enjoyed experiences which in the later period gave him hope of discovering or having revealed to him in nature those "manners" he had come to appreciate in Theocritus. The passage tells of how he had first come to appreciate, amid differing natural circumstances, man's true characteristics, his noblest traits:

[2] 27 Feb., 1799, in E. de Selincourt (ed.), *The Early Letters*, pp. 221–222.

By mists bewildered, suddenly mine eyes
Have glanced upon him distant a few steps,
In size a giant, stalking through thick fog,
His sheep like Greenland bears; or, as he stepped
Beyond the boundary line of some hill-shadow,
His form hath flashed upon me, glorified
By the deep radiance of the setting sun;
Or him I have descried in distant sky,
A solitary object and sublime,
Above all height! like an aërial cross
Stationed alone upon a spiry rock
Of the Chartreuse, for worship. Thus was man
Ennobled outwardly before my sight,
And thus my heart was early introduced
To an unconscious love and reverence
Of human nature; hence the human form
To me became an index of delight,
Of grace and honour, power and worthiness.

(1850; VIII, 264-281)

The landscape at the opening of "Tintern Abbey," one will recall, ends just at the moment when Wordsworth's attention turns from the rising smoke and the green scenery to thoughts of a hermit, whose fire the smoke might be coming from but who remains unseen, and in the light of the passage above, one sees that there was no need to bring the hermit bodily into the sketch, for everything necessary to know about the hermit can be read in the landscape—in its green harmony, its quiet and seclusion, and in the smoke that wreathes skyward, like a visible prayer connecting earth and heaven. The "manners" or modes of being—pleasure, grace, honor, power, and worthiness—which Wordsworth caught glimpses of in early life were men seen under propitious circumstances in opportune places; it was in the radiant light or mist, more than in the man himself, that he glimpsed pleasure, grace, and worthiness. The presence of a man was important, for it lent the moment and the visible beauty a point of human reference, but who the man was did not matter.

Another passage from *The Prelude* is in a way intermediate between the above passage and "Tintern Abbey," in that it both discusses and illustrates the genesis of the solitary:

> When from our better selves we have too long
> Been parted by the hurrying world, and droop,
> Sick of its business, of its pleasure tired,
> How gracious, how benign, is Solitude;
> How potent a mere image of her sway;
> Most potent when impressed upon the mind
> With an appropriate human center—hermit,
> Deep in the bosom of the wilderness;
> Votary (in vast cathedral, where no foot
> Is treading, where no other face is seen)
> Kneeling at prayers; or watchman on the top
> Of lighthouse, beaten by Atlantic waves;
> Or as the soul of that great Power is met
> Sometimes embodied on a public road,
> When, for the night deserted, it assumes
> A character of quiet more profound
> Than pathless wastes.   (1850; IV, 354–370)

The generative principle of character is personification, but it is neither wholly abstract nor wholly concrete personification; it is something between the two. Here the mood and the abstract preoccupation with solitude are presented first, then the figures that seem to epitomize outwardly the mode of being that the poet had been contemplating in the abstract. But the character, the mode of being, had to be half-created and half-*perceived*, and that is where place comes in. The dialectic of man and nature out of which true manners evolve is a dialectic in which, for Wordsworth, nature initiates things for the poet who is prepared by exhibiting the modes of being in all those special places it leads the poet to. In a remote place, even a deserted public way, nature will cause the spirit of solitude to put on flesh. Nor would it always matter if no actual person appeared, if the setting offered the poet visual or verbal symbols with which he could translate solitude into "solitary," hermitage into "hermit," or violet and star into "Lucy."

In Wordsworth's two fables of 1800, "The Waterfall and the Eglantine" and "The Oak and the Broom," no actual persons aside from Andrew, Wordsworth himself, appear, but modes of being do make their appearance. The waterfall is like the imagination—that is, a man under its sway—in its tyranny and usurpation, its tendency to obliterate lovely objects in nature as the imagination in its strongest moments obliterates sensation in man; the eglantine is like the fancy, lovely but fragile and evanescent, or like the life-in-sensation elegized in the "Lucy" poems; the oak is like the rational faculty, proud and querulous, but no reliable preceptor; and the broom is like love, which dozes while reason harangues and, wise in the lore of instinct—unlike the reason—does not stiffly oppose itself to natural forces. The deepest moral of these pieces is that the laws of our being pervade nature and that to know nature as Andrew does is to know man.

In other poems, of course, we encounter people, not simply objects, men such as one might expect to meet after reading the exerpts from *The Prelude* given above. In most cases the person stands in close relation to natural objects, however, that tend to spell out his special mode of being, his significance as a human being for us. The meeting with the gaunt man in "A narrow girdle of rough stones" is one such encounter. The fact that the man stands on a jut of land, cut off from the nearby fields and noisy harvesters, and that he stands over a "dead" lake is visually suggestive of the stoicism that is his apparent mode of being. He stands where heaven and earth meet, and his earth, the lake, "knew not of his wants" (line 72). His condition is pathetic, yet his tall, gaunt form, seen through a "veil of glittering haze" (which nature has no doubt glorified him with for the benefit of onlookers, in its role as initiator of the dialectic mentioned earlier) is impressive and moralizes the lovely images of the morning. What Wordsworth sees is not character in the ordinary sense, but a half-created, half-perceived revelation of the human condition, man in his search for a world that *knows* of his wants.

"Resolution and Independence" is a later study of a similar figure, or one might say a similar landscape-with-figure, for Wordsworth does not separate the old leech-gatherer in his mind from the physical circumstances under which the encounter took place, the moorish wastes and pools "bare to the eye of heaven" (line 54):

> In my mind's eye I seemed to see him pace
> About the weary moor continually.   (ll. 129–130)

The transfer of the epithet "weary" from the leech-gatherer to the moors speaks here, as it often does in Wordsworth, of the close connection between the mode of being and the place, and sometimes one cannot discern whether the epithet is really a transferred epithet. The

92

leech-gatherer shares his "life," his character, with the place, and that sharing is mirrored in the term "weary."

The young man from America in "Ruth" is one of the clearest examples, though not for us, perhaps, the most impressive, of Wordsworth's characterization during the experimental period of 1799–1800. The description of his appearance focuses on his colorful dress, the "hues of genius" in his visage, and his nodding feathers, in short, only that which refers us to his exotic place of nurture. It is the place, America, that finally reveals his character, for America, we find, is really a spiritual condition, being the place of hypnotic sensory engagement which is established in the poem as a threat to Ruth's moral being. It is necessary to oversimplify somewhat here, but, if the reader considers "Ruth" in relation to the "Lucy" poems, he will recognize perhaps that "Ruth" concerns the danger to the soul of a too total immersion in nature or sensation.[3] One could say in Ruth's case that the capacity to live in harmony with nature is "Nature's gentlest boon" (see "Strange fits of passion"), but that absolute naturalization can seal off the spirit and prevent moral growth, growth toward a fully human status. Ruth's young man epitomizes the sleep of nature, or sensation, and thus he moves for us to the center of the landscape he paints to allure Ruth:

> He spake of plants divine and strange
> That ev'ry day their blossoms change,
> Ten thousand lovely hues!   (ll. 49–51)

It is not only what he says, however, that places him amid these objects; Wordsworth's similes serve the same purpose:

[3] See the discussion of "Ruth" in Chapter II of the present study.

93

He was a lovely Youth! I guess
The panther in the wilderness
Was not so fair as he;
And when he chose to sport and play,
No dolphin ever was so gay
Upon the tropic sea.   (ll. 31–36)

The similes, like those in "The Danish Boy," exhibit an overbalance in favor of nature and interlock with the descriptions of America in such a way as to cause the young man to blend almost invisibly with the place. The place as a mode of being is developed through the motif of lawlessness worked into the following stanzas:

But, as you have before been told,
This Stripling, sportive, gay, and bold,
And, with his dancing crest,
So beautiful, through savage lands
Had roamed about, with vagrant bands
Of Indians in the West.

The wind, the tempest roaring high,
The tumult of a tropic sky,
Might well be dangerous food
For him, a Youth to whom was given
So much of earth—so much of heaven,
And such impetuous blood.

Whatever in those climes he found
Irregular in sight or sound
Did to his mind impart
A kindred impulse, seemed allied
To his own powers, and justified
The workings of his heart.

Nor less, to feed voluptuous thought,
The beauteous forms of nature wrought,
Fair trees and gorgeous flowers;
The breezes their own langour lent;
The stars had feelings, which they sent
Into those favored bowers.   (ll. 115–138)

Even in England, America reasserts itself in him, claims
its own, and causes him to desert Ruth. The governing
opposition of the poem is not so much Ruth and her young
man as the green nature that restores Ruth and the colorful,
wild savannas of America. Ruth and the young man are in
reality the exponents of the two landscapes and are among
the clearest representatives of Wordsworth's new approach
to manners, his most diagrammatic characters of place.

7

Concrete Metaphors

"Kindred"

John Jones ends his highly interesting discussion of Wordsworth's poetry of solitude and relationship by stating that Wordsworth

> ... is in the strictest sense a nature poet, in suit of the natural world, eager to converse "with things that really are." But the sense of nature poet, although strict, is not confining. He can say with the Pedlar, "I see around me things which you cannot see."[1]

For readers of Wordsworth, the Pedlar's statement and Jones's comments must bring more sharply into focus the question of how Wordsworth enables the reader to see what the Pedlar sees. Jones answers this question by pointing to the theme of solitude and relationship and by indicating how the circumstances under which perception occurs modify the perception itself. The question deserves, in addition, an answer from a more exclusively stylistic standpoint, for what one "sees" in Wordsworth is as much in evidence in the microscopic verbal texture of his verse

[1] Jones, *The Egotistical Sublime*, p. 109.

97

as it is in the larger and more dramatic episodes that Jones largely relies on to make his point.

What one often actually sees at the textural level in Wordsworth is a fact of nature which has been imaginatively modified in the light of a remembered human experience. The following phrases exemplify this, in that they cause natural objects to be viewed through the "glass" of human relationships, or human beings to be viewed through the glass of nature relationships: "violets in *families*,"² "the *brotherhood* of ancient mountains,"³ "a little *grove* of their own kindred,"⁴ "*friendships* with the streams and groves."⁵ The italicized words, it may be granted at the outset, are metaphors; yet it may be shown that they are not metaphors in quite the usual sense, because Wordsworth has eradicated, in some cases effectually and in some perhaps not, the lines separating the human and natural spheres that the two terms in each metaphor draw upon. For example, the poem containing the last phrase above ("To Joanna") broadly establishes a "life of things" which renders possible the kind of relationship between human beings and streams and groves which can logically be designated by the term "friendship."

Such instances abound in Wordsworth, to the extent that they would seem to be the result of an ingrained and abiding resistance to the practice of making casual metaphoric equations, combined, as it were, with a persistent habit of joining two nominally distinct contexts of experience in a single word. One is eventually obliged to

---

² "To a Sexton," l. 20.
³ "To Joanna," ll. 69–70.
⁴ "The Old Cumberland Beggar," ll. 113–114.
⁵ "To Joanna," l. 8.

consider each larger event in Wordsworth as a kind of iceberg, mostly submerged, and the metaphor as the mere visible peak that belies its bulk. A brief history of the word "kindred" in selected contexts, and an analysis of a very few other metaphors, may provide some notion of Wordsworth's resistance to the making of casual identifications, as well as of the way ostensibly metaphoric words in Wordsworth gradually acquire a clearly literal force.

One of the earliest of Wordsworth's revisions involving the word "kindred" is of its use in the middle portion of "lines left upon a Seat in a Yew-tree." The revision was apparently made sometime during the Racedown period. The recluse of the poem, it will be recalled, had turned to society but had gained no sense of kinship with his fellow men; yet his solitude did not quiet his pain, but instead made him more keenly aware than ever of the feeling of community he needed and seemed fated not to have. How nature intensifies the social instinct is of central importance in the poem and is treated in two different ways in the two versions. To all casual appearances the two versions differ hardly at all in their substance, but because of a transfer of the epithet "kindred" from "Beings" to "loveliness" the later version attaches the intensification of the social instinct more firmly to the immediate scene than does the earlier version, and thus it conspires to make of nature a more patently active contributor to his social anxiety. The earlier version reads—

Nor, that time,

When nature had subdued him to herself,
At the return of thought would he forget
Those *kindred Beings* to whose favoured minds
Warm from the labours of Benevolence

99

The world and man himself as lovely shewed
Then in the weakness of his heart he sighed
With mournful joy to think that others felt
What he must never feel [6] [Italics mine].

The published version reads—

                              Nor, that time,
When nature had subdued him to herself,
Would he forget those Beings to whose minds
Warm from the labours of benevolence
The world, and human life, appeared a scene
Of *kindred loveliness*: then would he sigh
Inly disturbed, to think that others felt
What he must never feel [Italics mine].   (ll. 34–40)

The phrase "as lovely shewed" points forward to the
stronger connection of the later version between the
perceived scene and the scene-in-thought of "the world, and
human life"; but "as lovely shewed" is not emphatic, and
as a result the experience tends to break down into two
parts—first the perception of the natural scene, and then
the thought of a human community. Hence the transfer of
"kindred," which brings more forcefully to our attention
the fact that the solitary is seeing "human life" in the
immediate scene before him!

That the solitary's perception of the scene and his
thoughts of human life were identical would seem to be
indirectly attested by the vision of the solitary in *The
Excursion* (II, 827–881), which appears to be an expanded
version of the kind of experience which the recluse has in
the Yew-tree lines. In *The Excursion* the landscape itself is

[6] *Poetical Works*, I, 93.

presented as containing for the solitary a vision of "the world, and human life":

> The appearance, instantaneously disclosed,
> Was of a mighty city—boldly say
> A wilderness of building.   (II, 834–836)

Here the man-to-nature metaphor "kindred loveliness" becomes a nature-to-man metaphor in "a wilderness of building," and the identification of humanity and natural scene, though implicit in both, is stronger in the latter metaphor. The identification in *The Excursion* is made still stronger by the description of individual clouds as temple, palace, and citadel (line 858), and by the explicit assertion—

> By earthly nature had the effect been wrought
> Upon the dark materials of the storm. (II, 846–847)

The solitary's mind, that is, was not freely associating, but was closely examining shapes and forms in nature. It would seem likely, then, that the Yew-tree recluse's vision of man is not to be separated from his perception of the lovely scene before him and that the conjunction of the two accounts for the borrowing of "kindred," which offers in the later version a closer linking of the perception and the vision.

While one would think of "kindred," used with "loveliness," as a metaphor, because it translates the natural into the human, in this case a qualification should be entered, for "kindred" does not here apply to two objects external to the mind of the solitary, but to a single object, on the one hand, and on the other, to the mind's idealized repetition of that object. It is still used in an extended sense, one might say,

and yet one is given no real basis for judging of its literalness: who is to say that an object outside the mind cannot be
literally "akin," in even the most basic, the genealogical,
sense, to the mind's idea of that object?

In the Yew-tree lines, one is assuredly free to view
"kindred" as a transferred, and thus metaphorical, epithet,
but, having considered the other possibility, one is better
prepared to appreciate the subtlety of its use in the last of
the "spots of time" (see *The Prelude*, XII, 287–335 and
XIII, 1–47). The passage that is relevant here tells of how
Wordsworth, when he was young, left his brothers behind
and climbed a crag to scout for horses that were to take
them home for the holiday. As he was straining for a sight
of the horses, nature seized the moment to etch in his mind
certain "collateral" forms that evoked in him the idea of
companionship. Like the term "kindred" in the Yew-tree
lines, the term "companions" in the following passage
would appear to be metaphoric, though only in the mildest
possible sense because the objects it refers to are physically
with him; even so, it is usually used, needless to say,
perhaps, to refer to people:

> I sate half-sheltered by a naked wall;
> Upon my right hand crouched a single sheep,
> Upon my left a blasted hawthorne stood;
> With those companions at my side, I watched,
> Straining my eyes intensely, as the mist
> Gave intermittent prospect of the copse
> And plain beneath.   (XII, 299–305)

The idea of companionship comes up twice again, once in
the stronger term "kindred" and again in the yet stronger
term "fraternal":

And, afterwards, the wind and sleety rain,
And all the business of the elements,
The single sheep, and the one blasted tree,
And the bleak music from that old stone wall,
The noise of wood and water, and the mist
That on the line of each of those two roads
Advanced in such indisputable shapes;
All these were *kindred* spectacles and sounds
To which I oft repaired [Italics mine]. (XII, 317–325)

Above all

Were re-established now those watchful thoughts
Which, seeing little worthy or sublime
In what the Historian's pen so much delights
To blazon—power and energy detached
From moral purpose—early tutored me
To look with feelings of *fraternal* love
Upon the unassuming things that hold
A silent station in this beauteous world [Italics mine].
(XIII, 39–47)

One begins to understand fully the incremental sequence here only by taking into account the intervening matter. Between the terms "companion" and "kindred," we are told of the death of Wordsworth's father, which seemed to him a kind of chastisement related to his experience on the crag. The later use of the term "kindred" offers a way of accounting for his feeling, if we choose to see a connection, in that the objects were prophetic: the naked wall with its bleak music, the crouching sheep, and the blasted hawthorne were deprived and melancholy things, as he was soon to be. The epithet "kindred" raises their status from one of incidental proximity to one of relatedness or kinship.

Between the terms "kindred" and "fraternal," the

narrative breaks off and we return to a later time, but there is no discontinuity in the underlying concern of the last part of Book XII and the opening lines of Book XIII. Such episodes as that on the crag, Wordsworth goes on to say, had taught him to "reverence a Power" that

> Holds up before the mind intoxicate
> With present objects, and the busy dance
> Of things that pass away, a temperate show
> Of objects that endure.   (XIII, 29–32)

The "show / Of objects" becomes the property of the "right reason," which is elsewhere associated with the imagination, the power of mind which answers to the reverenced power of nature; and the "show," as well as the "objects," like the powers of mind and nature, give promise of enduring. It is this later recognition of the significance of the sights and sounds on the crag that apparently induces Wordsworth to grant those objects the yet higher status of "fraternal" things, for he recognizes their origin to have been that power of nature which corresponds to the imagination. The sheep, the wall, the hawthorne, and so forth, were objects that nature held up before him and that his imagination, in its kinship or resemblance, was capable of singling out for remembrance and eventual comprehension.

The question of literalness here takes us even one step further, into the personification of XIII, 39–47. And the term "kindred" in "kindred spectacles and sounds" takes on an even more clearly literal force than it does in the Yew-tree lines, for here objects come to be for Wordsworth "unassuming things," that is to say dimly volitional things, and the thoughts to which they are related come to be "watchful," that is to say, again, on the threshold of volition. Such objects become, in short, "nature's living images,"[7] which in his mind "possess a kind of second life."[8] The living object, in this special sense of the term "living," and the living idea based on that object would logically have the same justification for being called "kindred" to one another, as do blood-related human beings. The alternatives are two: either one tends to accept the entire fabric of Wordsworth's experience as literal in this regard, or one tends to accept it as pervasively but mildly metaphoric. One can hardly consider its metaphors individually without losing a great deal, for the language everywhere works to support the literalness of the experiences it describes.

What is needed is a term to distinguish between the metaphor considered as a purely rhetorical figure of speech, one that is not descriptive of Wordsworth's practice, and the metaphor of continuous vision. The term I must use, the term "concrete metaphor," is not good enough, but it will provide some notion of the quality of the difference and help avoid inkhorn terms. The term "concrete metaphor," then, is meant to suggest that the verbal fabric of which "kindred" and such terms form a part enables "kindred" to function as a metaphor without the metaphor's loss of substantiality in one of its two terms. In the ordinary

[7] *The Prelude*, 1850, Book VI, l. 302. E. de Selincourt (ed.), *The Prelude*, rev. H. Darbishire (2nd ed.; Oxford: Clarendon Press, 1959), Book VI, l. 302.
[8] "The Brothers," l. 86.

metaphor we grant the substantiality of the tenor and the truth of the relationship, but we deny the substantiality of the vehicle, calling it figurative only; the word "kindred," as it is used in *The Prelude*, has been seen to function as a vehicle and yet not be "figurative." In Wordsworth the sensation and the idea, the tenor and the vehicle, are equally endowed with substance by their context. As there is an outward landscape in Wordsworth *and* an inward landscape, each in its own way substantial, so his metaphors tend to be in each of their referent areas substantial, for they invariably communicate between the two landscapes, between concrete thing and concrete idea.

"Vows"

Whether it is the result of a poetic faltering on Wordsworth's part or some inadequacy on our part as readers, certain passages in Wordsworth, while they persuade us of their importance to him, do not finally hand over their experiences in such a way that they can be shared. Even assuming that a reader is sympathetic and practiced in tracing in Romantic poetry the vagaries of the heart's holy affections, how is he to account for Wordsworth's taking of "vows" to poetry as a calling after a night of trivial amusement and upon stepping into the dawn (see *The Prelude*, IV, 307–338)? Certainly the two experiences, the trivial amusement and the self-dedication, are independently plausible, and one might even supply a connection between them, for example, the workings of a stern conscience; but, if we must suppose, we admit defeat, or the failure of the lines to supply the necessary connections among events so that we can sense their timeliness and share Wordsworth's feeling of urgency about them. A wide knowledge of his biography is of little help in this instance, for it appears that he had several similar moments of dedication.[9]

The possibility is worth exploring that the opacity of this experience (and perhaps some others like it) is related to Wordsworth's unusual metaphoric practice; that is, perhaps certain of the difficulties in his poetry may disappear if one adjusts his reading habits to account for the literal force of his words within the metaphorically heightened context of his language at large. It has not been considered, for example, that there is a metaphoric quality about the entire experience as it is recounted in Book IV, and that within that context the term "vows" may not refer to Wordsworth's *response* to the dawn scene, but to *the scene* itself as it substantially exists in his mind (in the sense of "inward landscape"). Upon seeing the dawn scene, Wordsworth exclaims later—

> I made no vows, but vows
> Were then made for me; bond unknown to me
> Was given.   (IV, 334–336)

The "vows," strange as it may seem to say, may have been the scene itself, a something given him by nature, a "solemn imagery" in precisely the sense of the lines:

[9] See the I. F. note to *An Evening Walk* (*Poetical Works*, I, 318–319); in it, Wordsworth indicates that his "poetical history" dates from a walk between Hawkshead and Ambleside, with the seeing of the sun through the branches of an oak. The scene is of course evening, not dawn. To attempt to sort out these comments might prove to be of some value, but in Wordsworth one experience blends with and reinforces another, until they cannot easily be separated, especially on the basis of comments he made so many years later.

The visible scene
Would enter unawares into his mind
With all its solemn imagery.
("There was a Boy," ll. 21–23)

If this were so, the term "vows," like the term "kindred" discussed earlier, would be more closely linked to the visual scene than one might have thought. It would prove to be, in short, not wholly literal but instead concretely metaphoric, for it would represent a convergence of thing and idea, scene and image, in a single word that expresses not a fanciful comparison but a fact, a literal description of what the scene became once it entered the mind.

There are ways of establishing a certain probability in this reading of the vows episode, ways which, when explored, reinforce in turn the hypothesis advanced here of an unusual metaphoric practice in Wordsworth. One can turn first to "There was a Boy," which offers a key to the vows episode, then examine the argument in *The Prelude* that leads into the episode, and finally examine earlier analogous lines, all in order to gain some perspective on his thought and expression. Used with caution, the comparative method can be fruitful in studying Wordsworth, for he revised and rewrote so extensively that it is sometimes difficult to distinguish between the revision and the new departure, though his language and imagery frequently make it clear that each experience forms the basis for two and sometimes more poetic renderings.

The remainder of the passage cited above from "There was a Boy," which includes the lines Coleridge claimed he would have recognized anywhere as Wordsworth's,[10] is

[10] Letter to Wordsworth, 10 Dec., 1798, in E. L. Griggs (ed.), *Collected Letters of S. T. Coleridge* (4 vols.; Oxford: Clarendon Press, 1956–1959), I, 266–267.

given a nuptial coloring by the addition to "solemn" of the description of the lake as receiving the sky into its bosom:

> the visible scene
> Would enter unawares into his mind
> With all its solemn imagery, its rocks,
> Its woods, and that uncertain heaven, receiv'd
> Into the bosom of the steady lake.　　　　(ll. 21–25)

"Uncertain," "receiv'd," "bosom," and therefore "steady" all contribute to the light personification, the germ of which is already present in the word "solemn." "Solemn" suggests a visually austere quality in the scene, but it is also the stem of the word "solemnity," which can denote a marriage ceremony. The word "solemn" and the phrase "uncertain heaven, receiv'd / Into the bosom of the steady lake" tend to reinforce one another and establish, on the one hand, a metaphoric color in the boy's inward image and, on the other hand, a literal force in the word "solemn" in its meaning of "solemnity" or ritual joining, for the mind has wed heaven and lake, and the word "solemn" denotes the ritual. Another poet might simply have spoken of a marriage of sky and lake, but in Wordsworth the transformation of the image does not result in our losing hold of the immediate visual facts—the steadiness of the lake, the uncertainty of the heavens, and the austerity of the scene as a whole.

The broader context of the vows episode in *The Prelude* indicates a certain correspondence between "There was a Boy" and the dawn episode that culminates in Wordsworth's receiving of vows. Wordsworth begins (IV, 307), pointedly addressing Coleridge, with an account of a night spent in idleness and dancing. If there is any connection between night and dawn, it is in the theme of love, for the night had been remarkable only because of

> ... here and there
> Slight shocks of young love-liking interspersed,
> Whose transient pleasure mounted to the head
> And tingled through the veins.   (IV, 316–319)

The pleasure of the dawn scene, on the other hand, affected not his head, but his heart:

> Ah! need I say, dear Friend! that to the brim
> My heart was full.   (IV, 333–334)

Moreover, the sequence of head to heart takes its place in a larger context in which Wordsworth argues for Coleridge's benefit that his present "inner falling off" need not necessarily bode ill for the great task of a philosophical poem (which Coleridge had been urging upon him); thus the specific theme of love has its implications with respect to that of poetic dedication, and the two themes of course merge in the receiving of vows. There is an interesting ebb and flow to the argument which indicates that Wordsworth is not firmly decided within himself about his inner falling off, but the dawn scene is magnificently affirmative and shows him strongly disposed to think of his present falling off as another prelude to a renewal of dedication from without, from nature. The high points of the argument are as follows:

> Nor less do I remember to have felt,
> Distinctly manifested at this time,
> A human-heartedness about my love
> For objects hitherto the absolute wealth
> Of my own private being and no more. (IV, 231–235)

> Yet in spite
> Of pleasure won, and knowledge not withheld,
> There was an inner falling off—I loved,
> Loved deeply all that had been loved before,
> More deeply even than ever; but a swarm
> Of heady schemes jostling each other, gawds,
> And feast and dance . . .
>
> . . . all conspired
> To lure my mind from firm habitual quest.
>
> (IV, 276–287)

> Far better had it been to exalt the mind
> By solitary study, to uphold
> Intense desire through meditative peace;
> *And yet, for chastisement of these regrets,*
> *The memory of one particular hour*
> *Doth here rise up against me* [Italics mine].
>
> (IV, 304–309)

What follows, the evidence to him of hope, is the account of the night of trivial amusements, followed by the moment of deep dedication coming from without, a renewal from nature. The vows passage, then, would seem to illustrate that a loose spending of poetic energies, a human-heartedness in his love, may be nothing to regret. His very prodigality of such times, when, secure of its joy,

> The heart luxuriates with indifferent things,
> Wasting its kindliness on stocks and stones,
> And on the vacant air,　　　　("Nutting," ll. 40–42)

might be the necessary giving of small gifts of love that signals nature to bestow upon him in return a blessing far in excess of his generosity. In "Nutting," the bower gives up to him its quiet being; here, nature gives him his vows.

III

In sum, the argument states that the wasteful "young love-liking" of the night hopefully corresponds to the time of wasteful kindliness in "Nutting" and his present human-heartedness, his inner falling off from the high task of writing his epic, for if it does, he may expect a renewal of his poetic dedication from nature. After his night given over to idle love-liking, Wordsworth steps directly into a dawn that is in a sense love writ large—not effervescent, but solemn:

>   Magnificent
> The morning rose, in memorable pomp,
> Glorious as e'er I had beheld—in front,
> The sea lay laughing at a distance; near,
> The solid mountains shone, bright as the clouds,
> Grain-tinctured, drenched in empyrean light;
> And in the meadows and the lower grounds
> Was all the sweetness of a common dawn—
> Dews, vapours, and the melody of birds,
> And labourers going forth to till the fields.
> Ah! need I say, dear Friend! that to the brim
> My heart was full; I made no vows, but vows
> Were then made for me; bond unknown to me
> Was given, that I should be, else sinning greatly,
> A dedicated Spirit.   (IV, 323–337)

Love is nowhere mentioned, but as in "There was a Boy," where the lake receives the sky in its bosom, here the brightness of the mountains answers to the light-drenched clouds, and the sweet, melodious foreground of the "common" dawn answers to the distant laughing sea. The scene as a whole is aesthetically knit by the light and joy that become, inwardly, the "vows," the "bond" that nature gives to Wordsworth.

"Vows" thus appears to be a concrete metaphor, a concrete articulation *and* idealization of the scene itself. In *The Recluse* one finds a similar concrete metaphor, namely the term "blended holiness," in a passage that begins, significantly, with the plea, "embrace me then, ye Hills ...."[11] Speaking of his chosen vale, Grasmere, Wordsworth says,

> No where (or is it fancy?) can be found
> The one sensation that is here ....
>
> . . . .
>
> 'Tis, but I cannot name it, 'tis the sense
> Of majesty, and beauty, and repose,
> A blended holiness of earth and sky.[12]

The effort to name the unnamable, which is called a "sensation" (that is to say, a thing both outside and inside the mind),[13] issues in the term "blended holiness." It is here attached to the earth and sky, but there is, here, the same inward-outward equivocation as there is in the sequence of "common" (in "all the sweetness of a common dawn" [*The Prelude*, IV, 330]) and "vows"; that is, while the terms "blended" and "common" would seem to refer to qualities in the outward scene, "holiness" and "vows" clearly introduce his feelings *about* the scene and thus obviously have to do with the inward, not the outward, landscape.

However, inasmuch as the inward landscape is visually like the outward landscape, all of the terms come to have

---

[11] *Poetical Works*, V, 317–318; l. 110.
[12] *Ibid.*, ll. 135–144.
[13] See the reference to C. C. Clarke, *Romantic Paradox*, in the Introduction of the present study (p. 2), and see *Romantic Paradox*, p. 25.

the same equivocal quality; yet they vary in degree, for "common" is more outward-oriented than "vows," one might say, so that the sequence becomes incrementally more and more inward. The term "blended holiness" is indeed precisely the missing middle term between "common" and "vows" that would have made "vows" much less problematic, for the sequence would then be "common," "blended holiness," and "vows," a clearer outward-to-inward progression. Such a sequence would have exhibited the same movement as does the sequence "companion," "kindred," and "fraternal" in the last of the "spots of time." The problem with "vows" noted at the beginning of this discussion may then be not necessarily a faltering on Wordsworth's part, for one would not have the dawn scene otherwise, but a lack of preparatory matter, not enough spreading out (for those who hold that there is too much already). A complex sequence requires time and space; to turn a landscape into a symbol before our eyes, the poet must work either very fast or very slowly.

"Home"

In a way, "Hart-leap Well" exists to propound two notions of home, one being the home represented by Sir Walter's elaborate pleasure-house, the other being that which the hart had enjoyed on the same site before it became a spot accursed, blighted by "the hand of man" (line 112). Although the word "home" does not appear, the shepherd's insight regarding why the spot was cursed by nature, and the entire second part of the poem, is an expansion of the shepherd's almost accidental use in a slightly metaphoric sense of the term "death-bed," which invokes the submerged metaphor of home; even though the word does not appear, it is the governing idea, more so than in some other poems where it does. Many of the poems in Volume II of the 1800 *Lyrical Ballads* are, at their deepest level of meaning, about the establishing of a suitable home in nature, but none more than "Hart-leap Well."

Perhaps the best way to illustrate the true force of the underlying idea of home in the shepherd's description of the hart's way of life is to contrast it with the description of Sir Walter's pleasure-house. The latter is called a "mansion" and a "great lodge," and, although Sir Walter had predicted that it would last "till the foundations of the mountains fall" (line 73), nature has decreed otherwise, for now "the Pleasure-house is dust" (line 169). The pleasure-house is clearly an instance, then, of a blending of "our pleasure or our pride / With sorrow of the meanest thing that feels" (lines 179–180), which Wordsworth in these final lines deplores for the reason that Sir Walter had built in a spirit of pride, to commemorate the sorrowful event of the hart's slaughter. The wider implications of the mansion in Wordsworth are made clearer in the fifth part of the Intimations Ode, where he speaks of our soul's home before our birth as a palace and of nature as a "homely Nurse" who tries to make us forget our former glory:

> The homely Nurse doth all she can
> To make her Foster-child, her Inmate Man,
> Forget the glories he hath known,
> And that imperial palace whence he came.
>
> (ll. 81–84)

The palace or stately home in Wordsworth appears to represent the soul's self-assertion as an alien being against nature's effort to accustom the soul to its new environment;

that is, it represents the soul's attempt to resume its imperial status through architectural splendor. If, however, the soul is to be acclimated to nature, to make its home

> ... in the very world, which is the world
> Of all of us,—the place where, in the end,
> We find our happiness, or not at all!
>
> (*The Prelude*, 1850, XI, 142–144)

it must give over its architecutral pride and submit to nature's lesson in "Hart-leap Well." The short inscription "Lines Written upon a Stone near a deserted Quarry" spells out the moral of "Hart-leap Well" in more explicit terms:

> Then peace to him
> And for the outrage which he had devis'd
> Entire forgiveness.—But if thou art one
> On fire with thy impatience to become
> An Inmate of these mountains, if disturb'd
> By beautiful conceptions, thou hast hewn
> Out of the quiet rock the elements
> Of thy trim mansion destin'd soon to blaze
> In snow-white splendor, think again, and taught
> By old Sir William and his quarry, leave
> Thy fragments to the bramble and the rose,
> There let the vernal slow-worm sun himself,
> And let the red-breast hop from stone to stone.
>
> (ll. 23–35)

The last few lines above touch on that other kind of home, the home enjoyed by the hart, which the shepherd has come to appreciate. How he comes to appreciate it leads

directly to the matter of how language works in Wordsworth. The shepherd is, first of all, sympathetic with the
hart; Sir Walter, because of his "forgivable" pride in the
chase, could not sympathize with the hart in the shepherd's
subtle way. Seeking a term that would both describe the
event in fact and convey his sympathy, the shepherd lights
upon the term "death-bed." The very word is like a flash of
insight that opens up a new perspective on the hart's
relationship to that now-barren spot:

> And in my simple mind we cannot tell
> What cause the Hart might have to love this place,
> And come to make his death-bed near the well.
>
> Here on the grass perhaps asleep he sank,
> Lull'd by this fountain in the summer-tide;
> This water was perhaps the first he drank
> When he had wander'd from his mother's side.
>
> In April here beneath the scented thorn
> He heard the birds their morning carols sing,
> And he, perhaps, for aught we know, was born
> Not half a furlong from that self-same spring.
>
> (ll. 146–156)

"Death-bed" is sufficiently common as to be no longer
metaphoric, but the shepherd's sympathy leads him to
revive its latent metaphoric force, for it brings him to a new
sense of the identity in suffering of man and beast, a new
understanding of the meaning of "inmate"; just as quickly
as this occurs, of course, and the lines between the human
and animal kingdoms is erased for him, the word "death-
bed" becomes literal for him in a new way and opens up for

him a world of surmise in which the hart is seen in human dimensions. Since his speculations are nowhere absurd or improbable, we come to accept the whole fabric of his surmise as literal in force, all the while recognizing the principle of transference everywhere at work. This is how the concretion of metaphor works and how language makes it possible, for the object contemplated (the hart) blends into the memory of a human experience through such words of commonly vague application as "inmate" and "death-bed." The term "home," which actually informs the shepherd's description, is precisely another such word, and it is employed by Wordsworth almost universally as a concrete metaphor, or at least exploited for its idiomatic acceptability in even the loosest of applications, as in—

> Though the torrents from their fountains
> Roar down many a craggy steep,
> Yet they find among the mountains
> Resting-places calm and deep.
>
> Though almost with eagle pinion
> O'er the rocks the Chamois roam,
> Yet he has some small dominion
> Which he no doubt calls his home.
>
> ("Song for the Wandering Jew")

Considering his method, one finds it odd that Wordsworth did not fall into banality at every turn.

The poem "Inscription for an Outhouse" develops "Hart-leap Well," in its contrasting of types of homes, through humor and light satire. We recognize in the following passage the type of home that Sir Walter's architect no doubt persuaded him to erect:

> he, the poor
> Vitruvius of our village, had no help
> From the great city; never on the leaves
> Of red Morocco folio saw display'd
> The skeletons and pre-existing ghosts
> Of beauties yet unborn.

In the latter part of the poem, a gentle humor disguises the theme which the shepherd had developed in all its apparent seriousness for Wordsworth; the fern becomes a "bed," the sheep a "household," and the opening of the shelter a "doorplace" giving on "fair sights, and visions of romantic joy," as though it were one of Shelley's all too clearly "imagined" ivory arcades.

"To M. H." describes a spot in a way that brings to mind the shepherd's description of the hart's home, and yet there is a curious reversion or "re-naturalization" of the domestic metaphors that appears to remove the notion of "home" almost out of the compass of its ordinary human connotations. The bed, for example, is a "bed of water," and the ordinary metaphoric movement of bower qua home is reversed in the phrase "plant his cottage." The human term thus seems to be given, then snatched away. These reversals may be viewed as exhibiting a subtle decorum that indirectly attests to Wordsworth's concern with close accuracy of observation: the place is unique, and its uniqueness is respected, not by a heaping up of descriptive detail, but by a seizing of its essential quality through imaginative contemplation. The essential quality which the imagination singles out is that the spot was "made by Nature for herself." The reversal of the metaphoric movement, which now assimilates the human to the natural, is in keeping with the scene's essential and unique quality. It is likely that

no merely descriptive detail, however select, could evince
the particular mood of the place so effectively as do its novel
metaphors.

"It was an April morning," like "Hart-leap Well,"
terminates an upward climb with a discovery of a "home"
in nature. Unlike the climb in "Hart-leap Well," however,
the climb in "It was an April morning" does not begin in
unmitigated tumult, nor does it end in an overshooting of
the mark, so to speak, in the form of an outrage against
nature such as the killing of the hart or the building of a
proud pleasure-house. At the opening of the poem, we find
that the rivulet, which is often in Wordsworth the poet's
alter ego, has spent its winter strength of voice and "soften'd
down into a vernal tone" (line 5). The entire lower landscape
in fact suggests a tamed strength or vigorous desire held in
check, for although the spirit of enjoyment and desire seems
to circle freely, it is muted by a "deep contentment in the
air" (line 13). The harmony between Wordsworth's mood
and the scene is further reflected in the shift from the
surplus of "various" and circling energies which appear to
be deflected and turned in upon themselves owing to
"hindrances that stood / Between them and their object"
(lines 11–12), to a corresponding "confusion" within
Wordsworth which appears to drive him up the brook. His
suggestion that he was "alive to all things and forgetting all"
(line 19) is another point of similarity, for the disorder of
immediate sensory distractions and forgetfulness, the lack
of a permanent and stable consummation amid a plethora of
hopes and wishes, is *his* "hindrance."

Upon coming to a dell in the glen, Wordsworth finds
himself amid sights and sounds that suggest for him an
order lacking in the scene below; the key to the orderliness

is that each thing strikes him as being like something else and that all the imagery seems to have a stability in its quality of stonelike permanence. Except for the "continuous" presences of the sound of the waterfall and the sounds issuing from the meadow below, the sensation of permanence is a reflexive insight, a perceiving of the mind's permanence which leads him to exclaim " 'our thoughts at least are ours' " (line 38), for the statement implies that even if the actual dell should change it will never change in his thoughts. Thus the earlier "forgetting all" (line 19) has been cancelled and a consummation of a kind has been achieved. In the light of the poem's pattern of desire and consummation and because he names the dell for Dorothy, it is surprising that F. W. Bateson does not draw our attention to it in his discussion of their love.[14]

Whatever subliminal implications the poem may contain, its primary import is its carefully developed theme of the mind's home in nature, a theme introduced explicitly only after the breaking off of the narrative, in the lines—

> Soon did the spot become my other home,
> My dwelling, and my out-of-doors abode.
>
> (ll. 40–41)

The probable reason for his putting off the idea of domicility so long is that, had he introduced it earlier, he might have obscured the fact that the dell is not simply a home, but a place especially suited for the *mind*. The dell is a middle ground between grove and waterfall, a fact suggestive neither of a total immersion in nature and sensation, nor of a totally visionary mode of existence. The dell is the mind's

[14] See Bateson, *Wordsworth: a Reinterpretation*, p. 148 ff.

true place in nature, for it is a place where the confusion of sensation gives way to an orderly and harmonious influence and where naked order and pure ideas, on the other hand, are clothed in delightful objects and sensations; it is in short a concrete metaphor for the way of life Wordsworth chooses for himself—the life of the poet, who clothes his truths in pleasurable objects and sensations.

"*Clothed*" *and* "*Naked*"

The growth of the mind beyond sensation and into thought, and the blessings and dangers attendant upon each stage of that development, have been touched on in various chapters of this study; it may come as no surprise, therefore, that the cluster of words having to do with clothing and nakedness is also closely related to this most central of themes in Wordsworth. The metaphoric value of this group remains quite constant, especially in *The Prelude, The Excursion,* and the later poetry; so little does it in fact depend upon the immediate context that in cases such as the following, one is justified in concluding that Wordsworth resorts to the use of his term, not as a concrete metaphor, but as a metaphor plain and simple:

> It seems the Eternal Soul is clothed in thee
> With purer robes than those of flesh and blood.[15]

> That change shall clothe
> The naked spirit, ceasing to deplore
> The burthen of existence. Science then
> Shall be a precious visitant.[16]

[15] "Brook, whose society . . . ," ll. 111–112.
[16] *The Excursion,* IV, ll. 1249–1252.

> Therefore with her hues,
> Her forms, and with the spirit of her forms,
> He clothed the nakedness of austere truth.[17]

> Nor am I naked of external things,
> Forms, images.[18]

The constancy of their metaphoric value, however, should alert us to the fact that in no instance is the metaphor simply plucked out of the air, the happy invention of the moment, but, on the contrary, that each is rooted in a single cosmology of being and extension, of thought and sensation; each supports an ethical vision, a vision that terminates the search for a delicate balance between the demands of the "naked spirit" and those of "flesh and blood." In the above instances of the metaphor, we are given the beneficial aspects of the life of sensation, for without the "hues" of sensation, we learn, the truth would be too austere to live with.

More affirmative of the life of thought and distrustful of the life of sensation are the following passages from *The Prelude*; only in the second is the clothing metaphor explicitly introduced, in the word "veil," but the gleaming arras of the first is but a slight variant of the metaphor:

> The surfaces of artificial life
> And manners finely wrought, the delicate race
> Of colours, lurking, gleaming up and down
> Through that state arras woven with silk and gold;
> This wily interchange of snaky hues,
> Willingly or unwillingly revealed,
> I neither knew nor cared for.   (III, 559–565)

[17] *The Excursion*, I, ll. 267–269.
[18] *The Prelude*, 1850, Book I, ll. 154–155.

>   when I left
> Our cottage door, and evening soon brought on
> A sober hour, not winning or serene,
> For cold and raw the air was, and untuned . . .
> .   .   .   .
>   . . . Gently did my soul
> Put off her veil, and, self-transmuted, stood
> Naked, as in the presence of a God.
>
> (IV, 142–145 and 150–152)

Much the same polarity is evident in all these uses of the clothing metaphor as was noted in "It was an April morning," although the emphasis in these is more clearly moral. From them we learn that it is bracing to the soul for it to put off its veil, to affirm itself, that is, in its knowledge of its origin and destiny, after having accommodated itself (though not too well) to nature. The ethical mode is to achieve in life, as in one's poetry, the middle ground of Emma's dell, a place where truth is clothed, yet where its form shines through.

The difficulty in this appears to be that man, unlike nature, has no self-regulating agency, so that crisis at one extreme or the other seems inevitable. The tendency toward ethical imbalance is perhaps the closest thing to original sin that one finds in Wordsworth, for it is clearly a condition that characterizes man from the outset, from his fall as a newborn child from paradise into nature. Nature, however, can be an instrument of grace for the man who is too righteously proud to immerse himself in a life of pure sensation and yet sufficiently humble to persevere in his reduced circumstances; for such a man, nature offers a garment to "clothe [his] naked spirit."

In Volume II of the 1800 *Lyrical Ballads*, the metaphors

of clothing and nakedness, like that of home, often remain submerged, but no less in force than they are in *The Prelude*. The "Lucy" poems, for example, may be thought to treat of a crossing-over from sensation to thought, for when Wordsworth treats of the life of sensation he almost invariably introduces the motifs of dream, light, color, and motion; the Lucy of "Three years she grew" thus clearly speaks to Wordsworth of a time

> . . . when meadow, grove, and stream,
> The earth, and every common sight,
> To me did seem
> Apparelled in celestial light,
> The glory and the freshness of a dream.
> ("Ode on Intimations of Immortality," ll. 1–5)

The introduction of the clothing metaphor in "apparelled" tells us that it is in the period of youth that the metaphor of clothing is likely to be introduced, for it must come prior to the fading of "celestial light" into the light of maturity, at which time the peculiar splendor of sensation falls away. By a characteristic Wordsworthian transference, it is Lucy who, in "A slumber did my spirit seal," is said no longer to see or hear, but it is implicitly Wordsworth for whom the "light of sense" has gone out (if we take into account the submerged metaphor of clothed), whether "with a flash that has revealed / The invisible world" (*The Prelude*, 1850, VI, 601–602) we do not know. There are indications that he *has* caught a glimpse of the invisible world, however, for the rocks, stones, and trees cannot be seen *in their diurnal motion* with the bodily eye alone!

In a way, the clothing metaphor does emerge in the word "seal" in "A slumber did my spirit seal." His spirit, sealed in stanza i, is implicitly unsealed (exposed or naked) in stanza ii. The sealing and unsealing extend the more usual idea of clothed and naked into their poem and provide yet another piece of evidence that stanza ii depicts the birth of thought, following upon the death of sensation, in Wordsworth and that Lucy is a projection of himself, a symbolic fiction.

"Three years she grew" repeats the sequence of the death of sensation followed by the birth of thought, and, again, what is in fact happening to Wordsworth is represented as happening to Lucy. Nature, in telling how it means to make Lucy its own, provides indirect hints as to what Lucy is when she is still living, but the language invokes the transformed Lucy by subtly dissolving her, by making her unvisualizable through a kaleidoscopic shifting from sense to sense: Lucy shall *feel* an over*see*ing power; though full of glee and active, she will possess the *balm* of *mute, insensate* things; the *motions* of the storm will *mold* her body; *sounds* will pass into her *face*; and finally, *delight* will rear her *form*. The many and unexpected transactions between Lucy and nature and between one sense and another tend strategically to bewilder the bodily eye and thus give birth to certain ideas of beauty that can only be described as abstract, having to do, that is, with thought rather than sensation. "Such thoughts," says Nature, "to Lucy I will give," and we are urged by what precedes Nature's remark to hypostatize "thoughts" by referring the term directly to those abstract beauties that nature shall have conferred upon Lucy. In short, Lucy will become "thoughts" of beauty for Wordsworth, conceptions of beauty from which most or all of the sensory co-ordinates have been systematically removed by nature. The clothing metaphor is again just below the surface, for in the end nature will have caused Lucy to "put on" thought and "put off" sensation, a phenomenon which has in fact happened in Wordsworth's own case.

The elegiac tone of the "Lucy" poems softens the shock of the crisis of imagination they are concerned with. In a way, that shock is not suppressed, for it is passed on to Ruth, Matthew, and Leonard Ewbank. Even "The Waterfall and the Eglantine" is a disguised re-enactment of the crisis, though the urgency of the crisis is diminished by Wordsworth's use of the fable. The metaphor of clothing and nakedness informs the basic opposition of the fable, and this time it breaks through to the surface in the words "shelter'd," "ornaments," and "deck" in the following lines:

> "And in the sultry summer hours
> I shelter'd you with leaves and flowers;
> And in my leaves now shed and gone
> The linnet lodg'd and for us two
> Chaunted his pretty songs when you
> Had little voice or none.
>   .   .   .   .   .   .
> Though of both leaf and flower bereft,
> Some ornaments to me are left—
> Rich store of scarlet hips is mine
> With which I in my humble way
> Would deck you many a Winter's day,
> A happy Eglantine!"   (ll. 35–40 and 45–50)

As mentioned earlier, the waterfall suggests the proud and tyrannous usurpations which the imagination sometimes brings down upon man, and the eglantine suggests the frail evanescence of the fancy, or sensation; in the present context the two can be foreshortened, the waterfall suggesting thought and the eglantine sensation, as indicated by the eglantine's remark to the waterfall, in a spirit of complaint, "but now proud thoughts are in your breast" (line 41). The eglantine, like Lucy, comes to grief, but not before stating in the above lines the case for the life of sensation. The fable as a whole strongly urges the preserving of a harmony between the eglantine and the waterfall, between thought and sensation:

> "Why should we dwell in strife?
> We who in this, our natal spot,
> Once liv'd a happy life!
> You stirr'd me on my rocky bed—
> What pleasure thro' my veins you spread!"
>
> (ll. 22–26)

Such harmony, pleads the eglantine, would assure at least a winter decked out in scarlet hips, a modicum of sensation, that is, in later life. Sensation, so the argument would go if carried beyond these confines, is, in limited amounts, a desirable protection (or one might say garment) against the absolute tyranny and usurpation of thought.

The note of distress that elsewhere accompanies the crisis of imagination is also absent in "Hart-leap Well," which treats of the crisis as an accomplished fact, a fact of history. The first part of the poem re-enacts the crisis, but almost ceremonially, in a full regalia of medieval trappings— knight, damsel, vassal, paramour, minstrel, and even falcon. Sir Walter's proud thought is to whet his spirit in the chase, and he and the hart together mutely conduct, on behalf of man and nature, the dialogue of waterfall and eglantine. The hart's death has consequences which Sir Walter could not have foretold, for it brings a curse upon the spot and obloquy upon the memory of Sir Walter in the thinking hearts of later generations of men. The cursed spot is significantly stripped of its garment of beauty so that it will be eloquent of "what we are, and have been" (line 174). The naked spot in Wordsworth is like an obliteration of sense data in nature, corresponding to the obliteration of sensation in the mind when it falls into an abyss of idealism, under the total sway of the imagination, so that what the naked spot in nature suggests is again that the pleasure-house was the expression of an alien spirit, of man's alien soul that, in its youth, finds all of nature a barren ground. Nature promises, however, that through mutual sympathy, which the shepherd has learned, man and nature, unlike the waterfall and eglantine, can achieve a *modus vivendi*—more than that, an "ennobling interchange" (*The Prelude*, 1850, XIII, 375). Looking toward the time when this will be, Wordsworth once more brings to the surface of his poem its submerged metaphor of clothing:

> Nature, in due course of time, once more
> Shall here put on her beauty and her bloom.
>
> (ll. 171–172)

It was noted at the beginning of the present discussion that the clothing and nakedness metaphors in *The Prelude* and *The Excursion* were metaphors in quite the usual sense. Such is not the case in certain of the shorter poems looked at here, for such terms as "put on," "seal," "deck," "ornament," and others like them, though they carry into their poems the idea of clothed and naked, have an aptness to their immediate contexts that makes them more concrete than those of Wordsworth's more discursive poetry, because in a sense they are more literal. They *both* depict and idealize, leaving no feeling that an "idea" has been imported into the local event; there is little of the fanfare of "the metaphor" about them. Yet they do import ideas, prior feelings and conceptions that can be traced in the warp and woof of the entire fabric of Wordsworth's considerable output of poetry, but especially in the poetry of the Goslar period and for a time thereafter.

Conclusion

Comparatively few of Wordsworth's metaphors are striking, but many are nevertheless memorable, for example,

> She seemed a thing that could not feel
> The touch of earthly years.

What makes them so is not their ingenuity, any more than their vehemence; it is their personifying of some unusual entity, a personification achieved with hardly any distortion or any gross improbability. Moreover, Wordsworth's finest imagery does not argue; it records. Something puts lines in our faces; to call it the *touch* of earthly years is to describe the indescribable, to fill in with high imagination the vacancy left by our abstractions. But high imagination— Wordsworth would in this case have insisted on calling it fancy—is not enough. For poetry to record and not simply imagine, it must do more than make comparisons: it must cause us to see that in reality all its comparisons are facts, facts that singly remain the objects of our fancy, but that all together and harmonious become the record of a vision. Wordsworth's vision was of a world where distinctions of abstract and concrete, animate and inanimate, and real and ideal remain only where the poet has not yet cast his glance, has not yet described things as they really are. In that world, the touch of earthly years is fact, not fancy.

The usually quiet metaphors in Wordsworth and the singularly consistent views of things he advances by means of them are the qualities which, if we discount rhythm, chiefly convince us of his sincerity and profundity.[1] The quietness of a metaphor is of course a relative matter, yet Donne's yoking of the idea of two souls to that of "stiffe twin compasses" contrasts sufficiently with Wordsworth's "the touch of earthly years" for us to acknowledge opposite tendencies.[2] Both kinds of metaphors can produce an effect of sincerity and profundity, but the strong metaphor usually introduces an element of irony or wit that in turn emphasizes the personal quality of the vision; the sincerity one detects beneath the wit, or that forges a vision out of the elements of irony, is an experienced, a sophisticated sincerity. Wordsworth's is of another sort; it is not personal in this sense, for, despite his "egotism," Wordsworth's poetry does not really dramatize the self so much as it makes use of the self in an impersonal way to dramatize things. His was to be the common or universal mind, and

[1] An important, richly suggestive study of the relationship between Wordsworth's poetry and the poetic criterion of sincerity is David Perkins, *Wordsworth and the Poetry of Sincerity* (Cambridge, Mass.: The Belknap Press of Harvard University Press, 1964); Perkins' method and my own differ, and so it is reassuring to find that we are in agreement in important respects; for example, Perkins states that with Wordsworth, "one feels that the symbolic becomes literal" (p. 195), a conclusion I have arrived at starting from a different area of concern.

[2] See Cleanth Brooks, "Irony as a Principle of Structure," in M. D. Zabel (ed.), *Literary Opinion in America* (New York: Harper, 1951), p. 735; Brooks contrasts Donne's and Wordsworth's ironic structures.

his poetry the voice that gives utterance to the thoughts of us all. Striking a note of almost Augustan self-denial, Wordsworth says,

> The poet thinks and feels in the spirit of human passions. How, then, can his language differ in any material degree from that of all other men who feel vividly and see clearly? ... Unless therefore we are advocates for that admiration which subsists upon ignorance, and that pleasure which arises from hearing what we do not understand, the Poet must descend from this supposed height [poetic diction]; and, in order to excite rational sympathy, he must express himself as other men express themselves.[3]

While directed primarily against what Wordsworth considered the most serious error of his time and earlier— the poetic diction of the many imitators of Pope, Thomson, and Gray, especially their bold but easy abstract personification—his pronouncement may be taken to militate as well, in its implicit mistrust of all extreme verbal tactics, against more recent practices in the idiosyncratic *or* manneristic use of strong metaphors, practices that until quite lately have been applauded by the poet's more or less specialized and sophisticated audience.

Several reasons for the return to stronger metaphor present themselves. One is the pride we take, if we share the modern poet's dark vision of man as an alien in nature, in observing a mind in its capacity to subdue nature, to subjugate by means of words that which threatens in other respects to annihilate it. That is, the bold metaphor dramatizes a self that is in one way superior to nature and assures

[3] 1802 Preface, in Brett and Jones (eds.), *Lyrical Ballads*, p. 255.

us all by proxy of our integrity in an indifferent and belittling universe. Another is the view in which to approximate the language of everyday speech is to risk banality. Wordsworth, too, had an alien vision, but he found in language a revealed affinity between man and nature, a means for narrowing, not widening, the gulf. This won him the title, among the younger aliens who did not see the part played by language in Wordsworth's reconciliation, of the "lost leader" (what they mainly noticed was the political conservatism which was a by-product of the reconciliation with nature). As for the risk of banality, that is of course a risk that every poet runs, whatever his theory of language may be. The alternative, aristocratic aloofness or withdrawal from the common idiom, may be the greater risk. The point is that Wordsworth largely avoided banality, that what he wrote is poetry; poetry, then, cannot be said to depend upon the strong metaphor. Where we must look to find the essential quality of his poetry is in its universally acknowledged intensity of emotion. Whereas Wordsworth argued for a common or natural language, he said nothing of being content with the flaccidity of feeling that characterizes the ordinary man's use of the language.

Again discounting rhythm, which may often be the primary contributing factor, emotion in Wordsworth may be traced to his applying a truism according to which, in the words of Quintilian,

> Too much care for our words . . . weakens the impression of emotional sincerity, and wherever the orator displays his art unveiled, the hearer says, "The truth is not in him."[4]

[4] *Institutio Oratoria*, trans. H. E. Butler, IX.iii.102; III, 507.

The effect of feeling and truth in this sense is achieved, as this study is designed to show, in no easy manner, for it often entails a rather elaborate avoidance of devices that will be recognized as such. One must strive to turn all of one's figures into what Quintilian calls "figures of thought," as distinct from figures of language, speech, or what not. Accordingly there may result a striving for an "inevitable" quality, a naturalness of expression related to the English Augustan hope of finding the words to say "What oft was thought, but ne'er so well expressed."

On the other hand, Wordsworth clearly purges the ideal of naturalness and simplicity of all sophism before applying it himself; rather, he does not "apply it"—it is his way, for he opposes "poetic device" to truth. Such phrases as "an eye made quiet," "the life of things," or "a man who does not move with pain, but moves / With thought," since they do not jar us into thinking of them as devices, are not merely evocative of a mood of truthfulness, they are the truth itself, a seeing of things "as they really are." The poet, then, does not make metaphors; he discovers the veritable homologies among things. Discussing his own metaphor in the lines "Shall I call thee Bird, / Or but a wandering Voice?" Wordsworth says,

> This concise interrogation characterizes the seeming ubiquity of the voice of the cuckoo, and dispossesses the creature almost of a corporeal existence; the Imagination being tempted to this exertion of her power by a consciousness in the memory that the cuckoo is almost perpetually heard throughout the season of spring, but seldom becomes an object of sight.[5]

[5] 1815 Preface, in *Poetical Works*, II, 437.

The metaphor must respect the facts of observation. Without a theory of the mysteriousness of mere things and the faculty in man capable of plumbing the mystery, Wordsworth's view of metaphor might have turned his poetry into scientific prose in meter. But he had such a theory, one that assumed the poet's involvement with things, not as they strew his path, but as they rise up through unconscious selection (the agency of nature) and call his imagination into play. When that happens, the poet has no need of "wit," the capacity of impromptu comparison-making, for things then speak an inarticulate language of their own, a symbolic utterance which the imagination comprehends:

> "Smoothe verse, inspired by no unlettered Muse,"
> Exclaimed the Sceptic, "and the strain of thought
> Accords with nature's language;—the soft voice
> Of yon white torrent falling down the rocks
> Speaks, less distinctly, to the same effect." [6]

Although in the final analysis Wordsworth does not deal in figures of speech, but as it were in truth, it is still profitable to single out his figures and describe them from a traditional rhetorical point of view, bearing in mind the different assumptions in each case. One way in which we profit is in seeing how Wordsworth puts older rhetorical categories to work for him. By beginning a poem, for example, with language that clearly respects personification by avoiding it and then by introducing personification almost unnoticeably, he establishes a proximity in our minds between man and nature which blunt personification could not

[6] *The Excursion*, VI, ll. 522–526.

effectuate. Another example is his occasional use of a strong metaphor to gain a special effect. To understand this figure, we must first appreciate the fact that the usual metaphor in Wordsworth is of a quiet ("natural" or idiomatic) order, as in "some *injury* done to sickle, flail, or scythe," where "injury" is like the common metaphor of mistake, or in "'the sun itself / Has scarcely been more *diligent* than I,'" where the metaphor "diligent" tells of how passion can render our everyday speech metaphoric without our really intending to engage in "metaphor." Such are the anti-rhetorical figures (figures, that is, which are not to be thought of as "ornaments") which Wordsworth claims the poet will discover if he chooses his subject and his language judiciously:

> . . . if the Poet's subject be judiciously chosen, it will naturally, and upon fit occasion, lead him to passions the language of which, if selected truly and judiciously, must necessarily be dignified and variegated, and alive with metaphors and figures.[7]

Against this background of quiet or natural metaphor, Wordsworth's few strong metaphors seem almost to have invisible quotation marks around them, or in some way seem to imply especially strong feeling or symbolic significance, as in,

> And then she sang!—she would have been
> A very nightingale,

[7] 1802 Preface, in Brett and Jones (eds.), *Lyrical Ballads*, pp. 248–249.

or as in,

> Then Nature said, "A lovelier flower
> On earth was never sown."

Where strong metaphors abound, the listener grows insensitive to the shades of meaning that they can communicate when used as Wordsworth uses them, and for that matter as Milton, his master in the cautious use of strong metaphor, uses them.[8]

Is Wordsworth to be considered, then, as simply a linguistically conservative poet in the sense of wishing to turn back the clock, to antedate in his poetry the "gaudy and inane phraseology" of his time? He is, of course, but he does not quite return in his poetry to a supposed one-for-one relationship between words and their referents, to a supposed transparency of language that once allowed things to speak for themselves, that made use of none of the opacities of artifice.[9] There is an approach to this kind of transparency in the increased literalness in Wordsworth and in his strict descriptive exactitude, but his language on the whole has as its point of reference an inward landscape, one already tinctured with feeling, modified in its transposition from external nature to the inward eye of the poet. As mentioned earlier, his is a poetry of vision, not mere

[8] Like his distaste for glitter, Wordsworth's disuse of the strong metaphor is traceable, it seems to me, to Milton, who uses "glitter" (in the sense of heavy rhetorical ornament) mainly in connection with Eve and Satan. What was surely logical strategy in Milton becomes even more clearly a matter of truth to nature in Wordsworth. The affinities between Milton and Wordsworth in this regard deserve more attention than they have received.

[9] See the opening four paragraphs of Wordsworth's Appendix on Poetic Diction, in *Poetical Works*, II, 405–406.

description; its world is a world so modified already that in it, sickles are literally "injured." Thus, whereas Wordsworth avoids the strong metaphor, he exploits the latent metaphoric element in words of all kinds, the element that renders them suitable for describing not simply things, but things and their correspondences, one to the other, particularly things we think of as either animate or inanimate, but which their correspondences reveal to belong to a single realm of being.

The purpose of drawing the human realm and the realm of nature into closer proximity in our thinking is the purpose that apparently governs all of Wordsworth's figures isolated in this study, from paradox to metaphor. Those words that for us imply a division between that which is sentient and that which is not undergo an enlargement of meaning in Wordsworth, and his figurative techniques are his means of enlarging their meanings in accordance with his vision. This singleness of function of all the figures makes it more difficult than usual to separate them. For instance, the word "injury," used with sickle, may be taken for metaphor. If, however, we associate it with other words in "Michael" that function in much the same way—the *aged* utensil, *diligent* sun, winds that *devise* work, and hours that *come* and *go*—we see that metaphor and personification are one and the same device. Examples of this kind of overlapping occur in every poem, of course, but the singular fact in "Michael" is that *all* of its figures overlap with personification in just the same way, and this puts the matter in a somewhat different light.

It becomes gradually clearer to the reader of Wordsworth that certain of our traditional rhetorical divisions are in his case not applicable and that the underlying reason for it is that the rhetorical divisions themselves in some instances rest on an assumed discontinuity between the animate and inanimate realms of being, an assumption that is not in accord with Wordsworth's view of man and nature. To illustrate the difficulty, suppose we were to define, as we tend to do, one species of the metaphor as a verbal transaction between the animate and the inanimate realms or contexts. What, then, would become of it, in a rhetorical sense, where the animate and inanimate comprise but a single context? Obviously it would become literal statement, for sickles *could be injured* and young girls could be flowers. This situation, which only partially obtains in Wordsworth, should make it clearer why Wordsworth exercises great caution in using strong metaphors. In such a situation, personification, too, would cease to be a figure, for hills and fields could literally be called beings. Synecdoche, and the figure that reverses personification in the leech-gatherer's case, would also become meaningless distinctions the moment it became literally true that one's feet and not one's self did the struggling, and that the leech-gatherer was indeed "propped" and did not lean; that is, all figures that reverse personification would likewise cease to mean what they ordinarily do mean—that life has been taken away—because if all things have life, then life itself and all distinctions grounded in it must be redefined.

This "merging of contexts" is offered for illustration only, for it holds only partially true in Wordsworth, as was mentioned. Its purpose is to show the need for flexibility in the setting up of rhetorical categories. Wordsworth apparently perceived the limitations of the old categories, for up to a point he exploits them, not as a sophist might, but as one might who believed he had seen a life in things and who believed that a creative approach to language would be one that approached it not as a set of fixed conventions, but as the medium of continuous revelation.

The preservation of his sanity is not the only reason one could supply to explain why Wordsworth did not exploit his insight further than he does, for were his two contexts of man and nature wholly merged they would not preserve his concept of man and the spirit of nature as two separate beings. There are in fact four contexts to be observed in Wordsworth. Both man and nature have souls at their center, so to speak, and material adjuncts at their periphery. The spiritual eye, the bodily eye, the spirit of nature, and the world of natural objects—these are the four realms, or contexts. Two of these contexts, those of the bodily eye and of the world of natural objects, characteristically merge to form one context in the course of the poetic narration, leaving us finally with three contexts. The soul of man and the soul of nature stand apart from one another and from that realm in which the sensed object and the sensation blend and form an alphabet of symbolic images, the medium through which the two aloof souls commune.

The "concrete metaphor," the word or figure that fuses thought and thing, is Wordsworth's means for merging the two contexts of bodily eye and natural object and for creating his symbolic verbal images. Earlier, the term "concrete" was used only in connection with a few figures, but now it can be seen that the principle involved in those few figures is in force in all of the figures examined in this study. Also, the term "concrete" was earlier referred to as inadequate, and the reason for that may also be clear now: memories, ideas themselves, remain concretions in Wordsworth, just as his landscapes remain intact even after they move into the mind's eye. The only truly abstract thing in Wordsworth is that speechless, imageless moment of pure feeling, that prelude or postlude to communion that occupies the pauses of the poem, its silences. Ideas are still things that the soul looks upon, as it looks upon natural objects; the idea and the object thus have a closer bond in Wordsworth than they may for us, and with language to bind them still closer, through an evincing of the laws that govern both, the idea and the object become inseparable in the poetic image, that is, the object of meditation that lets us into the Wordsworthian communion of man and nature through the poem.

Bibliography

BOOKS

ABERCROMBIE, LASCELLES. *The Art of Wordsworth.* London: Oxford University Press, 1952.

ABRAMS, MEYER H. *The Mirror and the Lamp: Romantic Theory and the Critical Tradition.* London: Oxford University Press, 1953.

———— (ed.). *English Romantic Poets: Modern Essays in Criticism.* New York: Oxford University Press, 1960.

ANDERSON, ROBERT (ed.). *The Works of the British Poets.* 14 vols. London, 1795.

ARTHOS, JOHN. *The Language of Natural Description in Eighteenth-Century Poetry.* ("University of Michigan Publications in Language and Literature," Vol. XXIV.) Ann Arbor: University of Michigan Press, 1949.

AUBIN, ROBERT A. *Topographical Poetry in XVIII-Century England.* New York: Modern Language Association of America, 1936.

BARFIELD, OWEN. *Poetic Diction: A Study in Meaning.* Revised 2nd ed. New York: McGraw-Hill, 1964.

BARSTOW, MARJORIE L. [MRS. GREENBIE]. *Wordsworth's Theory of Poetic Diction: A Study of the Historical and Personal Background of the Lyrical Ballads.* New Haven: Yale University Press, 1917.

143

BATESON, FREDERICK W. *Wordsworth: a Reinterpretation.* Revised 2nd ed. London: Longmans, Green & Co., 1956.

BEACH, JOSEPH WARREN. *The Concept of Nature in Nineteenth Century English Poetry.* New York: Macmillan, 1936.

✓ BEATTIE, JAMES. *Essays on Poetry and Music, Etc.* 3rd ed. London, 1779.

BEATTY, ARTHUR. *William Wordsworth, His Doctrine and Art in Their Historical Relations.* 2nd ed. ("University of Wisconsin Studies in Language and Literature," No. 24.) Madison: University of Wisconsin Press, 1927.

BLAIR, HUGH. *Lectures on Rhetoric and Belles Lettres.* 2 vols. London, 1783.

BLOOM, HAROLD. *The Visionary Company: A Reading of English Romantic Poetry.* New York: Doubleday & Co., 1961.

BOSKER, AISSO. *Literary Criticism in the Age of Johnson.* The Hague: J. B. Wolters' Uitgevers-Maatschappij, N. V., 1930.

BOWRA, SIR CECIL M. *The Romantic Imagination.* Cambridge, Mass.: Harvard University Press, 1949.

BRADLEY, A. C. *Oxford Lectures on Poetry.* London: Macmillan, ✓ 1909.

BROOKE-ROSE, CHRISTINE. *A Grammar of Metaphor.* London: Secker & Warburg, 1958.

BROOKS, CLEANTH. *The Well Wrought Urn: Studies in the Structure of Poetry.* New York: Reynal & Hitchcock, 1947.

✓ BROUGHTON, LESLIE N. *The Theocritean Element in the Works of William Wordsworth.* Halle: Max Niemeyer, 1920.

BUSH, DOUGLAS. *Mythology and the Romantic Tradition in English Poetry.* Cambridge, Mass.: Harvard University Press, 1937.

✓ CAMPBELL, GEORGE. *The Philosophy of Rhetoric.* Edited by L. F. BITZER. Carbondale: Southern Illinois University Press, 1963.

CLARKE, COLIN C. *Romantic Paradox: an Essay on the Poetry of Wordsworth.* New York: Barnes & Noble, 1963.

COLERIDGE, S. T. *Biographia Literaria, with his Aesthetical*

Essays. Edited by J. SHAWCROSS. 2 vols. Oxford: Clarendon Press, 1907.

———. *Collected Letters of S. T. Coleridge*. Edited by E. L. GRIGGS. 4 vols. Oxford: Clarendon Press, 1956–1959.

———. *The Poetical Works of S. T. Coleridge*. Edited by E. H. COLERIDGE. 2 vols. Oxford: Clarendon Press, 1912.

CONGLETON, JAMES E. *Theories of Pastoral Poetry in England, 1684–1798*. Gainesville, Florida: University of Florida Press, 1952.

COOPER, LANE. *A Concordance to the Poems of William Wordsworth*. London: Smith, Elder & Co., 1911.

DANBY, JOHN F. *The Simple Wordsworth: Studies in the Poems, 1797–1807*. New York: Barnes & Noble, 1961.

DAVIE, DONALD. *Articulate Energy: an Inquiry into the Syntax of English Poetry*. London: Routledge & Kegan Paul, 1955.

———. *Purity of Diction in English Verse*. London: Chatto & Windus, 1952.

DEANE, CECIL V. *Aspects of Eighteenth Century Nature Poetry*. Oxford: Basil Blackwell, 1935.

DRAPER, JOHN W. *The Funeral Elegy and the Rise of English Romanticism*. New York: New York University Press, 1929.

DURLING, DWIGHT L. *Georgic Tradition in English Poetry*. New York: Columbia University Press, 1935.

EMPSON, WILLIAM. *Seven Types of Ambiguity*. 2nd ed. London: Chatto & Windus, 1949.

FERRY, DAVID. *The Limits of Mortality: An Essay on Wordsworth's Major Poems*. Middleton, Conn.: Wesleyan University Press, 1959.

FINK, ZERA S. (ed.). *The Early Wordsworthian Milieu: A Notebook of Christopher Wordsworth with a few Entries by William Wordsworth*. Oxford: Clarendon Press, 1958.

FOAKES, R. A. *The Romantic Assertion: A Study in the Language of Nineteenth Century Poetry*. New Haven: Yale University Press, 1958.

FRIEDMAN, ALBERT B. *The Ballad Revival: Studies in the Influence of Popular Ballads on Sophisticated Poetry*. Chicago: University of Chicago Press, 1961.

GARROD, HEATHCOTE WILLIAM. *Wordsworth: Lectures and Essays*. Oxford: Clarendon Press, 1923.

GEROULD, GORDON HALL. *The Ballad of Tradition*. Oxford: Clarendon Press, 1932.

HANSON, LAWRENCE. *The Life of S. T. Coleridge: The Early Years*. New York: Oxford University Press, 1938.

HARPER, GEORGE MCLEAN. *William Wordsworth, His Life, Works and Influence*. 2 vols. London: John Murray, 1916.

HARTLEY, DAVID. *Observations on Man, his Frame, his Duty, and his Expectations*. 2 vols. London, 1791. (First published in 1749.)

HARTMAN, GEOFFREY H. *The Unmediated Vision: an Interpretation of Wordsworth, Hopkins, Rilke, and Valéry*. New Haven: Yale University Press, 1954.

————. *Wordsworth's Poetry, 1787–1814*. New Haven: Yale University Press, 1964.

HAVENS, RAYMOND D. *The Mind of a Poet: A Study of Wordsworth's Thought with Particular Reference to "The Prelude."* Baltimore: Johns Hopkins Press, 1941.

HAZLITT, WILLIAM. *Lectures on the English Poets, and Spirit of the Age*. Edited by A. R. Waller. London: J. M. Dent, 1910.

HENLEY, ELTON F. and STAM, DAVID H. (compilers). *Wordsworthian Criticism, 1945–59: An Annotated Bibliography*. New York: New York Public Library, 1960.

HIRSCH, E. D., JR. *Wordsworth and Schelling: A Typological Study of Romanticism*. New Haven: Yale University Press, 1960.

JAMES, D. G. *Scepticism and Poetry: An Essay on the Poetic Imagination*. London: Allen, 1937.

JONES, HENRY JOHN FRANKLIN. *The Egotistical Sublime: A History of Wordsworth's Imagination*. London: Chatto & Windus, 1954.

JOSEPH, SISTER MIRIAM, CSC. *Shakespeare's Use of the Arts of Language*. New York: Columbia University Press, 1947.

KAMES, HENRY HOME (LORD). *Elements of Criticism*. Edited by A. MILLS. New York, 1838. (First published in 1762.)

KNIGHT, G. WILSON. *The Starlit Dome: Studies in the Poetry of Vision*. London: Oxford University Press, 1941.

KNIGHT, RICHARD PAYNE. *An Analytical Inquiry into the Principles of Taste*. London, 1805.

KROEBER, KARL. *The Artifice of Reality: Poetic Style in Wordsworth, Foscolo, Keats, and Leopardi*. Madison: University of Wisconsin Press, 1964.

———. *Romantic Narrative Art*. Madison: University of Wisconsin Press, 1960.

LAMB, CHARLES and MARY. *The Letters of Charles and Mary Lamb*. Edited by E. V. LUCAS. 3 vols. New Haven: Yale University Press, 1935.

LANGBAUM, ROBERT W. *The Poetry of Experience: The Dramatic Monologue in Modern Literary Tradition*. London: Chatto & Windus, 1957.

LEAVIS, F. R. *Revaluation, Tradition and Development in English Poetry*. London: Chatto & Windus, 1936.

LEGOUIS, ÉMILE. *The Early Life of William Wordsworth, 1770–1798: A Study of "The Prelude."* Translated by J. W. MATTHEWS. London: J. W. Dent & Sons, 1921. (First published in 1896.)

LINDENBERGER, HERBERT. *On Wordsworth's "Prelude."* Princeton: Princeton University Press, 1963.

LOGAN, JAMES V. *Wordsworthian Criticism: A Guide and Bibliography*. Columbus, Ohio: Ohio State University Press, 1947.

McKENSIE, GORDON. *Critical Responsiveness: A Study of the Psychological Current in Later Eighteenth-Century Criticism*. ("University of California Publications in English," Vol. XX.) Berkeley: University of California Press, 1949.

MARSH, FLORENCE. *Wordsworth's Imagery: A Study in Poetic Vision*. New Haven: Yale University Press, 1952.

MEYER, GEORGE W. *Wordsworth's Formative Years.* ("University of Michigan Publications in Language and Literature," Vol. XX.) Ann Arbor: University of Michigan Press, 1943.

MILES, JOSEPHINE. *The Continuity of Poetic Language: Studies in English Poetry from the 1540's to the 1940's.* ("University of California Publications in English," Vol. XIX.) Berkeley: University of California Press, 1951.

———. *Eras and Modes in English Poetry.* Berkeley: University of California Press, 1957.

———. *Pathetic Fallacy in the Nineteenth Century: A Study of a Changing Relation Between Object and Emotion.* ("University of California Publications in English," Vol. XII, No. 2.) Berkeley: University of California Press, 1942.

———. *Renaissance, Eighteenth-Century, and Modern Language in English Poetry: A Tabular View.* Berkeley: University of California Press, 1960.

———. *Wordsworth and the Vocabulary of Emotion.* ("University of California Publications in English," Vol. XII, No. 1.) Berkeley: University of California Press, 1942.

MONK, SAMUEL H. *The Sublime: A Study of Critical Theories in XVIII-Century England, 1674–1800.* New York: Modern Language Association of America, 1935.

MOORMAN, MARY. *William Wordsworth: A Biography. The Early Years, 1770–1803.* Oxford: Clarendon Press, 1957.

———. *William Wordsworth: A Biography. The Later Years, 1803–1850.* Oxford: Clarendon Press, 1965.

NICOLSON, MARJORIE HOPE. *Mountain Gloom and Mountain Glory: The Development of the Aesthetics of the Infinite.* Ithaca: Cornell University Press, 1959.

PERKINS, DAVID. *The Quest for Permanence: The Symbolism of Wordsworth, Shelley, and Keats.* Cambridge, Mass.: Harvard University Press, 1959.

———. *Wordsworth and the Poetry of Sincerity.* Cambridge, Mass.: The Belknap Press of the Harvard University Press, 1964.

Piper, Herbert W. *The Active Universe: Pantheism and the Concept of Imagination in the English Romantic Poets.* London: Athlone Press, 1962.

Potts, Abbie F. *Wordsworth's "Prelude": A Study of Its Literary Form.* Ithaca: Cornell University Press, 1953.

Powell, Annie E. (Mrs. Dodds). *The Romantic Theory of Poetry. An Examination in the Light of Croce's Aesthetic.* New York: Longman's, 1926.

Quintilian, Marcus Fabius. *Institutio Oratoria.* Translated by H. E. Butler. 4 vols. London: William Heinemann, 1922.

Richards, Ivor A. *Coleridge on Imagination.* London: Kegan Paul, 1934.

Robinson, Henry Crabbe. *Correspondence with the Wordsworth Circle, 1806–1866.* Edited by E. J. Morley. 2 vols. London: Oxford University Press, 1927.

Smith, Elsie. *An Estimate of William Wordsworth by His Contemporaries, 1793–1822.* Oxford: Basil Blackwell, 1932.

Stallknecht, Newton P. *Strange Seas of Thought: Studies in Wordsworth's Philosophy of Man and Nature.* Revised 2nd ed. Bloomington, Ind.: University of Indiana Press, 1958.

Taylor, William. *Historic Survey of German Poetry.* 3 vols. London, 1830.

Tuveson, Ernest L. *The Imagination as a Means of Grace: Locke and the Aesthetics of Romanticism.* Berkeley: University of California Press, 1960.

Ullmann, Stephen. *Language and Style.* New York: Barnes & Noble, 1964.

Wain, John (ed.). *Contemporary Reviews of Romantic Poetry.* New York: Barnes & Noble, 1953.

Warren, Robert Penn (ed.). *The Rime of the Ancient Mariner.* New York: Reynal & Hitchcock, 1946.

Wasserman, Earl R. *The Subtler Language: Critical Readings of Neoclassic and Romantic Poems.* Baltimore: Johns Hopkins Press, 1959.

WELLEK, RENÉ. *History of Modern Criticism.* Vol. II: *The Romantic Age.* New Haven: Yale University Press, 1955.

WORDSWORTH, DOROTHY. *The Journals of Dorothy Wordsworth.* Edited by E. DE SELINCOURT. 2 vols. Oxford: Clarendon Press, 1952.

WORDSWORTH, WILLIAM. *Poems in Two Volumes, 1807.* Edited by HELEN DARBISHIRE. 2nd ed. Oxford: Clarendon Press, 1952.

———. *The Poetical Works of William Wordsworth.* Edited by E. DE SELINCOURT and HELEN DARBISHIRE. 5 vols. Oxford: Clarendon Press, 1940–1949. (Volume II re-issued by Helen Darbishire in 1952.)

———. *The Prelude, or the Growth of a Poet's Mind.* Edited by E. DE SELINCOURT, revised by HELEN DARBISHIRE. Oxford: Clarendon Press, 1959.

———. *The Prose Works of William Wordsworth.* Edited by W. A. Knight. 2 vols. London: Macmillan, 1896.

———. *Wordsworth's Literary Criticism.* Edited by NOWELL C. SMITH. London: Henry Frowde, 1905.

WORDSWORTH, WILLIAM, and COLERIDGE, S. T. *Lyrical Ballads, 1798.* Edited by H. LITTLEDALE. London: Oxford University Press, 1924.

———. *The Lyrical Ballads, 1798 and 1800.* Edited by R. L. BRETT and A. R. JONES, New York: Barnes & Noble, 1963.

WORDSWORTH, WILLIAM and DOROTHY. *The Early Letters of William and Dorothy Wordsworth.* Edited by E. DE SELINCOURT. Oxford: Clarendon Press, 1935.

———. *The Letters of William and Dorothy Wordsworth: The Middle Years.* Edited by E. DE SELINCOURT. 2 vols. Oxford: Clarendon Press, 1937.

YEATS, WILLIAM BUTLER. *The Collected Poems of William Butler Yeats.* New York: Macmillan, 1951.

ARTICLES

BARTHES, ROLAND, "L'imagination du signe," in *Essais critiques* (Paris: Editions du seuil, 1964), pp. 206–212.

BREWSTER, PAUL G., "The Influence of the Popular Ballad on Wordsworth's Poetry," *Studies in Philology*, XXXV (1938), 588–612.

BROOKS, CLEANTH, "Irony as a Principle of Structure," in M. D. ZABEL (ed.). *Literary Opinion in America*. New York: Harper, 1951. Pp. 735–737.

BURCKHARDT, SIGURD, "The Poet as Fool and Priest," *English Literary History*, XXIII (1956), 279–298.

CAMPBELL, OSCAR J., and MUESCHKE, PAUL, "Wordsworth's Aesthetic Development, 1795–1802," University of Michigan Publications in Language and Literature, Vol. X. Ann Arbor: University of Michigan Press, 1933. Pp. 1–59.

DE MAN, PAUL, "Symbolic Landscape in Wordsworth and Yeats," in R. A. BROWER and R. POIRIER (eds.). *In Defense of Reading: a Reader's Approach to Literary Criticism*. New York: E. P. Dutton & Co., 1962. Pp. 22–38.

EMPSON, WILLIAM, "Basic English and Wordsworth," *Kenyon Review*, II (1940), 449–457.

———. "'Sense' in *The Prelude*," *Kenyon Review*, XIII (1951), 285–302.

GÉRARD, ALBERT S., "Dark Passages: Exploring 'Tintern Abbey,'" *Studies in Romanticism*, III (1963), 10–23.

———. "Of Trees and Men: The Unity of Wordsworth's 'The Thorn,'" *Essays in Criticism*, XIV (1964), 237–255.

GROB, ALAN, "Wordsworth's 'Nutting,'" *Journal of English and Germanic Philology*, LXI (1962), 826–832.

HARPER, GEORGE McLEAN, "Coleridge's Conversation Poems," in M. H. ABRAMS (ed.). *English Romantic Poets: Modern Essays in Criticism*. New York: Oxford University Press, 1960. Pp. 144–157.

HARTMAN, GEOFFREY H., "Wordsworth's 'Descriptive Sketches' and the Growth of a Poet's Mind," *Publications of the Modern Language Association*, LXXVI (1961), 519–527.

————. "Wordsworth, Inscriptions, and Romantic Nature Poetry," in F. W. HILLES and HAROLD BLOOM (eds.). *From Sensibility to Romanticism: Essays Presented to Frederick A. Pottle.* New York: Oxford University Press, 1965. Pp. 389–413.

KNOWLTON, E. C., "The Novelty of Wordsworth's 'Michael' as a Pastoral," *Publications of the Modern Language Association,* XXXV (1920), 432–436.

KROEBER, KARL, "The Reaper and the Sparrow: A Study in Romantic Style," *Comparative Literature*, X (1958), 203–214.

MAYO, ROBERT, "The Contemporaneity of the *Lyrical Ballads,*" *Publications of the Modern Language Association,* LXIX (1954), 486–522.

MILES, JOSEPHINE, "Wordsworth and Glitter," *Studies in Philology*, XL (1943), 552–559.

MONK, SAMUEL H., "Anna Seward and the Romantic Poets: A Study in Taste," in E. L. GRIGGS (ed.). *Wordsworth and Coleridge: Studies in Honor of George McLean Harper.* Princeton: Princeton University Press, 1939. Pp. 118–135.

NOYES, RUSSELL, "Wordsworth and Burns," *Publications of the Modern Language Association,* LIX (1944), 813–832.

PARRISH, STEPHEN M., "Dramatic Technique in the *Lyrical Ballads,*" *Publications of the Modern Language Association,* LXXIV (1959), 85–98.

————. "'The Thorn': Wordsworth's Dramatic Monologue," *English Literary History*, XXIV (1957), 153–163.

PATER, WALTER, "Wordsworth," in *Appreciations.* London: Macmillan, 1889. Pp. 39–64.

PERCY, WALKER, "Metaphor as Mistake," *Sewanee Review*, LXVI (1958), 79–99.

POTTLE, FREDERICK A., "The Eye and the Object in the Poetry of Wordsworth," *Yale Review*, XL (1950), 27–43.

RADER, MELVIN M., "Presiding Ideas in Wordsworth's Poetry," in University of Washington Publications in Language and Literature, Vol. VIII, No. 2. Seattle: University of Washington Press, 1931. Pp. 121–216.

RANSOM, JOHN CROWE, "William Wordsworth: Notes Toward an Understanding of Poetry," *Kenyon Review*, XII (1950), 498–515.

RYSKAMP, CHARLES, "Wordsworth's *Lyrical Ballads* in Their Time," in F. W. HILLES and HAROLD BLOOM (eds.). *From Sensibility to Romanticism: Essays Presented to Frederick A. Pottle.* New York: Oxford University Press, 1965. Pp. 357–372.

SHACKFORD, MARTHA H., "Wordsworth's 'Michael,'" *Sewanee Review*, XXXI (1923), 275–280.

TRILLING, LIONEL, "The Immortality Ode," in *The Liberal Imagination.* New York: Viking Press, 1950. Pp. 130–158.

WILLEY, BASIL, "Wordsworth and the Locke Tradition," in *The Seventeenth Century Background: Studies in the Thought of the Age in Relation to Poetry and Religion.* London: Chatto & Windus, 1934.

WIMSATT, W. K., "The Structure of Romantic Nature Imagery," in M. H. ABRAMS (ed.). *English Romantic Poets: Modern Essays in Criticism.* New York: Oxford University Press, 1960. Pp. 25–36.

Index